THE ART AND IMAGINATION OF
LANGSTON HUGHES

R. Baxter Miller

THE UNIVERSITY PRESS OF KENTUCKY

Publication of this volume was made possible in part by
a grant from the National Endowment for the Humanities.

Editorial and Sales Offices: The University Press of Kentucky
663 South Limestone Street, Lexington, Kentucky 40508-4008
www.kentuckypress.com

10 09 08 07 06   5 4 3 2 1

The Library of Congress has cataloged the hardcover edition as follows:
Miller, R. Baxter
    The art and imagination of Langston Hughes / R. Baxter Miller.
        p.   cm.
    Bibliography: p.
    Includes index.
    ISBN 0-8131-1662-7
    1. Hughes, Langston, 1902–1967—Criticism and interpretation. 2. Afro-Americans in
literature. I. Title.
PS3515.U274Z684   1989
818'.5209—dc19
89-5645
ISBN-10: 0-8131-9152-1
ISBN-13: 978-0-8131-9152-2

For ELSIE BRYANT MILLER (1915–1979)
Mother, Christian, and Elementary School Teacher.

For more than twenty years she fought cancer
And finally she passed,
But she was never beaten
Because she had the "Crystal Stair" within.

And for Marcellus C. Miller (1916–2000)
Father, Science Teacher, and Long Distance Runner

CONTENTS

Acknowledgments   vii

Abbreviations   ix

Introduction to the Paperback Edition   x

Introduction to the Original Edition   1

1. "For a Moment I Wondered"
The Autobiographical Imagination   8

2. The "Crystal Stair" Within
The Apocalyptic Imagination   33

3. "Deep like the Rivers"
The Lyrical Imagination   47

4. "Oh, Mind of Man"
The Political Imagination   67

5. "I Heard Ma Rainey"
The Tragicomic Imagination   99

Conclusion   119

Notes   125

Selected Bibliography   135

Index   144

ACKNOWLEDGMENTS

I am grateful to many organizations and scholars for assistance during the past thirty-one years. Quite invaluable have been the Beinecke Rare Book and Manuscript Library at Yale University, the Schomburg Center for Research in Black Culture in Harlem, New York City, and the Free Library of Philadelphia, as has the Mainline consortium of collections for Villanova University, Haverford, Swarthmore, and Bryn Mawr colleges, and the University of Pennsylvania. The Vivian G. Harsh Collection in the Carter G. Woodson branch of the Chicago Public Library helped me to review the drafts and galleys of *The Big Sea*. The James D. Hoskins Library of the University of Tennessee at Knoxville assisted me by acquiring rare books through interlibrary loan. Updated research benefited from archives in the Ilah Dunlap Little Memorial Library at the University of Georgia.

Other scholars have aided me in fact and thought. Faith Berry and Arnold Rampersad read parts of the manuscript for this book with a keen eye. After Charles H. Nichols directed my attention to the literary history of the Harlem Renaissance, Richard K. Barksdale gave helpful advice about focus and style. Blyden Jackson brought me closer to Hughes's fondness for dramatic comedy in fiction. Other fellows in the Langston Hughes Society discussed numerous points at great length.

Among the institutions and organizations that provided me with a forum in which to test various premises over the years, I am grateful to the Modern Language Association and the College Language Association, as well as to Emory University and the University of Pennsylvania. Special thanks go to LeMoyne College, which invited me to present a reading of Hughes's political imagination as a part of the Black Scholar Lecture Series. In 1975 the National Endowment for the Humanities assisted my research with the award of a summer fellowship; the Better English Fund, established by John C. Hodges in the Department of English at the University of Tennessee, provided several summer grants from 1977 through 1985. And, though the bulk of my work as a National Research Council/Ford Foundation Senior Fellow (1986-87) would go to a forthcoming monograph, "Fall of Camelot: New Chicago Renaissance from Wright to Fair," that grant gave me invaluable time to hone the final revisions for this book as well.

Finally, I thank Akin, my son, especially for helping me to relax and enabling me to return with new energy for the drive toward publication.

Portions of this book were published earlier, and I am grateful for permission to reprint them here in somewhat revised form. Parts of chapter 1 appeared as "'Even After I Was Dead': The Big Sea—Paradox, Preservation, and Holistic Time," Black American Literature Forum 11, no. 2 (Summer 1977), copyright © 1977, Indiana State University; "'For a Moment I Wondered': Theory and Symbolic Form in the Autobiographies of Langston Hughes," Langston Hughes Review 3 (Fall 1984), copyright © 1984, The Langston Hughes Society; and my essay on Hughes for the Dictionary of Literary Biography, vol. 51. Chapter 2 appeared as "'No Crystal Stair': Unity, Archetype and Symbol in Langston Hughes's Poems on Women," Black American Literature Forum 9, no. 4 (Winter 1975), copyright © 1975, Indiana State University. Some lines from the new introduction are revised from "Reinvention and Globalization in Hughes's Stories," MELUS 30, no. 1 (Spring 2005) © MELUS, The Society for the Study of Multi-Ethnic Literature of the United States, and the New Historical Guide to Langston Hughes © Oxford University Press.

ABBREVIATIONS

Throughout both the notes and text, the following abbreviations are used for the most frequently cited editions of works by Langston Hughes.

AYM *Ask Your Mama: 12 Moods for Jazz.* New York: Knopf, 1961.

BS *The Big Sea: An Autobiography.* New York: Knopf, 1940.

GMR *Good Morning Revolution,* ed. Faith Berry. New York: Lawrence Hill, 1973.

FW *Fields of Wonder.* New York: Knopf, 1947.

JC *Jim Crow's Last Stand.* Atlanta, Ga.: Negro Publication Society of America, 1943.

NS *A New Song.* New York: International Workers Order, 1938.

PL *The Panther and the Lash: Poems of Our Times.* New York: Knopf, 1967.

SP *Selected Poems of Langston Hughes.* New York: Knopf, 1959.

WB *The Weary Blues.* New York: Knopf, 1926.

WF *The Ways of White Folks.* New York: Knopf, 1934; Vintage, 1971.

WW *I Wonder as I Wander: An Autobiographical Journey.* New York: Rinehart, 1956.

INTRODUCTION TO THE
PAPERBACK EDITION

Langston Hughes knew that the written life and life of writing are ever incomplete, for authors must subsume what they learn. By revising insights for new appeals to new generations, they restructure the fine designs. If they are honest, they admit where they have erred.

The last decade of Hughes studies benefits from the critical emergence of Donna Akiba Sullivan Harper (*Not So Simple* 1995) and solid contributions by Joseph McLaren (*Langston Hughes, Folk Dramatist in the Protest Tradition, 1921–1943* 1997). Especially the children's work (Dianne Johnson) and the political writings (Christopher De Santis) round out a completeness of the oeuvre. Gregory Woods, pushing the envelope of sexual orientation, points toward a previously closeted inquiry that the late Melvin Dixon, my Brown University doctoral associate and intellectual friend, once urged me to pursue. I am not so sure that Hughes wanted us to go there.

By 2026 literary criticism and theory on Hughes's life and work will enter a second century of inquiry. Then it will be the primary work of the current and earlier decades that will have facilitated such new horizons. For years, during the seventies and eighties, Houston A. Baker Jr. and others perceived clearly the way that a lack of fundamental texts limited the reach of African American criticism and theory. Even the most well-meaning and best-trained scholars could not do research in a textual vacuum. Today, with the definitive edition of *The Collected Works of Langston Hughes* in sixteen volumes recently completed, the magnificent series from the University of Missouri Press marks a historical moment in basic research on Langston Hughes. Equally important, the outpouring of preceding contributions encourages anew the kind of systematic exegesis and formal celebration of creative text, highlighting a richly deserved delight for Hughes enthusiasts.

So much was already going on during the decade in which the hardback of this issue appeared. The 1980s marked a timely renaissance in Hughes's reputation. A Langston Hughes study conference at Joplin, Missouri, in March 1981, helped inspire the founding of the Langston Hughes Society, in Baltimore, Maryland, on June 6 of that year. After a joint meeting with the College Language Society in April 1982, the society became, in 1984, the first group focused on a black author to become an affiliate of the Modern Language Association. In the fall of 1988, Raymond R. Patterson directed, at the City College of the City University of New York, "Langston Hughes: An International Interdisciplinary Conference," one of the most satisfactory tributes ever paid the author. Shortly afterward, a public television release, similarly titled, reaffirmed the high place of Hughes among the most celebrated national poets. More than a dozen renowned scholars and artists reassessed Hughes's contributions to the reshaping of American voices and visions.

Crucial texts are finally available for the first time. Arnold Rampersad and David Roessel researched a chronological *Collected Poems* (1994); Akiba Sullivan Harper complemented such fine detective work with *Short Stories* (1996). Christopher C. De Santis edited the collection of essays entitled *Langston Hughes and the* Chicago Defender (1995). For the new century, Susan Duffy has contributed *The Political Plays of Langston Hughes* (2000), and Emily Bernard a comparative edition, *Remember Me to Harlem: The Letters of Langston Hughes and Carl Van Vechten, 1925–1964* (2001). Altogether the contributions make for probably the most significant outpouring of basic research on Hughes since his death at Polyclinic Hospital in New York City on May 22, 1967.

Meanwhile, the brilliant scene recounted by Hughes at the close of 1937 has become a closure on his previous journey to Paris in 1922–1923. In the earlier instance, his gifted rendering ranges in ten chapters across forty-seven pages on France. During a rite of spring love, a prominent African businessman, who is father to Anne Coussey (the narrator's fictive Mary), dispatches a doctor-friend to summon the daughter home to London. On the way with Hughes to visit his place for the last time, she buys a paper cone full of *fraises des bois* that they eat together, seated in a gabled window overlooking the chimneys of Paris. While dipping strawberries into each other's cream, they are very *tristes* (sad), regretting the loss of sanctuary (a metonym for café), free from financial worry as from fathers. The coachman drives them back across the Seine, the rooftops gleaming reddish brown over the Parisian woods. "Arrêtez," he says to the horse, hence a French stopping of time. By the time he speaks to the horse again—"allons," the figuring of sex and death—Mary's departure from sanctuary is complete.

In *The Big Sea* (1940), Hughes recounts his 1923 trip to New York to attend a performance of Ibsen's *The Lady from the Sea* by the famous Italian actress Eleonora Duse (1858-1924). Frequently the poet had heard about the enchantment that stirred the human spirit. He had read about her in Gabriele D'Annunzio's *The Flame of Life* (1900) in which she seemed a virginal Juliet on the "dusty roads of Italy" (130-31). Though a serious illness in 1909 had dimmed her radiance, she entered the stage of the Metropolitan Opera House of New York to huge applause. By the end of the routine, writes Hughes, she seemed "just a tiny little old woman, on an enormous stage, speaking in a foreign language, before an audience that didn't understand. After a while, behind me some of the people began to drift out and it was not so crowded. . . . Before it was over, there was plenty of room." It is the obligation of performer and voyeur to blend into the textual moment. Both creativity and perception help shape the artistic experience. The autobiographer observes that the performer's theatrical magic has shrunk to a small voice, but her failure can never be hers entirely. Her personal decline seems to foreshadow the fate of the Jazz Age itself.

By the end of the twenties, later as a student at Lincoln University in Pennsylvania, Hughes finished a campus sociology project which showed that 63 percent of the nearly all-black student body preferred an all-white faculty. When he encountered a famous alumnus on campus, his findings offended the old man so much that the elder walked away. The autobiographer writes, "I looked at him crossing the campus, famous, well-to-do, the kind of man the gradu-ation speakers told us to look up to" (309-10).

"Young man, suppose I told the truth to white folks," the elder had begun. But echoes of great nineteenth-century abolitionists sounded in the autobiographer's memory: "I began to think back to Nat Turner, Harriet Tubman, Sojourner Truth, John Brown, Fred Douglass—folks who left no buildings behind them—only a wind of words fanning the bright flame of the spirit down the dark lanes of time." So there are the dual dimensions of space and time, of slavery and freedom. Literary inspiration emerges as a blowing fire. Conse-quently, enlightenment of the writer seems to provide a radiance magically without consumption. Into the vacated space of academic protocols—the Booker T. Washington legacy of racial accommoda-tion—the storyteller inscribes his own freed text and writes the tale of freedom rather than theorizing about it. He completes his sym-bolic rite (write) of purgation.

In the lead article for *Black American Literature Forum* (Summer 1977) and subsequent revisions, I overlooked the way that the years in Paris of 1923-1938 became for Hughes a trope across time and space set against the backdrop of African American folk life. By 1925 Hughes would return to the Harlem Renaissance. Perhaps it was sim-ply time for him to go home. Though I would recognize his tendency to do so in *The Art and Imagination of Langston Hughes* (1989), my complete awareness of the Parisian figures would not appear until a subsequent critical analysis of *I Wonder as I Wander* (1956), the sec-ond autobiography. A critical reading of the earlier work, *The Big Sea* (1940), had not revealed some telling patterns in the autobiographies. Several keys to understanding developed through the subsequent readings of *I Wonder as I Wander*. Nearly a generation ago, my intrigue with Hughes's figures of the café and the walkway had not captured the critical imagination. Today such explorations have proved re-markably rewarding.

Meanwhile, the popular novella "Father and Son," one of his most enduring fictions, provokes new readings. The storyteller nego-tiates a discrepancy between history and Time, between 1900, when the story might well take place, and an imaginative future date. The

narrator, expressing "The day that ends our story," looks forward to
the death of the revolutionary protagonist Bert Norwood. For the
moment, we project a reasonable time for the eagerly anticipated
closure of the tale. But the resolution of civil rights in the nation
and world has no expected date. A reference to *documented events*
(the story) marks the era of the Depression while an unfulfilled goal
of African American freedom points to a limitless *process in time*.
The story for Bert Lewis Norwood will end soon, but the tale of African American freedom will proceed indefinitely. The tragic deaths
of Bert and his brother Willie provide an illusory closure to the text,
for the story of African American freedom will conclude only at the
finishing of Time. By expressing the immediate occurrence in present time, the writer represents a re-creative process as always happen-
ing *now*. Much of the new fascination with Hughes might be for such
wild leaps in location and time.

My newest interpretations return us to the primary texts. Scholarly revelations derive from the rearranging of images on the Hughes
literary landscape. So many works become intertextual while prepar-
ing for others. It's as if we are ever moving pieces on a game board,
testing fresh angles of new placements at new geographical locations.
Meanwhile, the game board itself increases its range. In short,
Hughes's literary world grows as we do.

His narrators express a need for solitude to write; but somehow
they know that the writer's social responsibility intrudes on personal
privacy. By the close of his literary world, he surely knows that Word-
sworth's Romanticism has died long ago. Since his African American writers usually share their landscape with others such as news
reporters, dancers, or artists, their visions are communal. Even in
kinship, they claim their own distanced moments in time and space.
Though his narrators are rooted in the same historical world, they
exist almost magically beyond it.

His literary window on the Americas and the Caribbean prefig-
ures the imagined Paris of the twenties and thirties even as the image
fades into the Harlem of the fifties. It's a delightful tableau that
works. Though the literal journey takes place across national land-
scapes, his literary site actually expresses the writer's memory. What

he really writes about is *positioning* himself to the great cities and great monuments, his stance toward diverse peoples who inhabit diverse places. He reveals the apparently sacred bonds of community that bind fellows as the historical world collapses around them. His narrators situate themselves in particular places at particular times. His greatness takes shape as the structuring of synchronic history and diachronic time within the immediate space of a narrative event.

I have admired the way that the musical and verbal languages in *Ask Your Mama* (1961) complement each other. Today I would add that the page centers locate us in historical scenes from 1850 to 1961. But the musical and verbal margins—the page frames—locate us rather in ever-shifting moments of Time. By creating a tension between the verbal center and the musical margin, Hughes asks for an ironic resolution of contrasts. He voices modernity.

As the years go by, the defining properties of modernism are so much more easily recognized. By the publication of *Montage of a Dream Deferred* (1951), *Laughing to Keep from Crying* (1952), and *Ask Your Mama* (1961), he was experimenting with a bebop poetics and narrative streams of consciousness. By the sixties, he had certainly advanced beyond the decadent romanticism of the early century. These days I would hope to evince a greater precision of inquiring into the interconnectedness through which space and time function in his work.

In 2002 it was exciting to discover another clue to the writer's journey. His story about a Cuban spy in Havana during the rule of the Liberal Party leader Gerardo Machado y Morales from November 1924 until August 1933 initiates a great trope: "A mile away on the Malecon—for I [narrator] had continued to *walk along the sea wall—I looked* at my *watch* and saw *the hour* approaching *seven*, when I was to meet some friends at the *Florida Cafe. I turned to retrace* my steps. In *turning*, whom should *I face* on the sidewalk but the little old man! Then I became suspicious. He *said nothing* and *strolled on* as though he had not *seen* me. But when *I looked back after walking* perhaps a quarter mile toward the center, there he was a *respectable distance behind*" (italics mine).

Particularly during the journey or *walk* down the seashore, the traveler *looks* into the meaning of the *hour*. Meanwhile, the spy who follows him lacks his gift for words. Hughes responds to the artistry through which we engage history. Beyond the human moment of comfort and fraternity (café), we *turn* to *face* history. And it is our conscientious *turning* that makes the writer and us so perceptively suspicious about political reality. The newspaper editor Carlos sits in the café with a cousin, Jorge the poet, a dancer named Mata (reminiscent of Sylvia Chen in Hughes's own life), and an African American writer.

Later, in the Haiti of "Old Man Durand," a child listens to a tale about Toussaint L'Ouverture, the old coachman who emerged as Haitian liberator from 1794 to 1804. During his administration, a local citadel was built to safeguard the country in case the colonizing French ever decided to return. It was, of course, the Romantic Age. In 1802 Napoleon had proposed to reinstitute slavery in the Caribbean nation. Flashbacks make for highly effective temporal shifts between past and present. Returned into modern time, the narrator observes a boy's woodwork ("Popo's Tray"): "It is finished, Uncle Jacques. . . . It's finished, Old Man Durand. Just look." It's almost as if Haitian elders had written books:

> "Since this is your first," Uncle Jacques said, "you may carry it home and give it to Mamma Anna. Tell her to take good care of it. Tell her to remember that it was your first piece of work in my shop. When you are older you will make many beautiful things, many much finer than this tray; but there will never be another first one. For that reason the first one is precious."

The denouement finishes with the family journey to the lighthouse off the Haitian harbor. When the seekers have climbed the hill under the branches—there beneath the almond trees and tall oaks—they see water set against the high cliffs: "The lighthouse was still a good distance ahead, and Papa Jean and Uncle Jacques were walking steadily." Ever on the human journey, the child of African ancestry—and therefore the human species—ascends the hill of vision, the metonym of the child's flying kite. During the beating of the Haitian drums, the journey leads *to the lighthouse*.

From *The First Book of Negroes* (1952), through *The First Book of Rhythms* (1954), *The First Book of Jazz* (1955), and *The First Book of the West Indies* (1956), to *The First Book of Africa* (1960), Hughes traces the African journey to Timbuktu, Mali, near the end of the sixteenth century. Beyond the African American figures, he points to those of African ancestry who speak diverse languages throughout the world—Brazil (Portuguese), Caribbean (French), Gulf of Mexico (Native American languages), the Black Sea (Russian), and Guiana (Dutch). To Hughes, the "rhythms of life" connect idioms, for the universe seems to be an almost living organism that connects all people and things. Today his definition of a "blue" note still proves instructive, as does his outlining of the basic elements of jazz (syncopation, improvisation, drums, rhythm, blue note [off note, glissando, slur], and tone color). His tables of musicians and countries facilitate the researching of a player's particular instrument or a writer's nation, forcing a neat compartmentalization to make us see beyond national boundaries.

In all volumes in the Missouri series, a six-page chronology about the writer's life and work comes standard. Four primary sections in the omnibus volume include contributions from the *Brownies' Book* (1920–1921), which was the children's insert into the *Crisis; The Dream Keeper and Other Poems* (1932), at least fifteen memorable poems, of which at least twelve are reprinted from Hughes's first volume, *The Weary Blues* (1926); and *Popo and Fifina, Children of Haiti* (1932) along with stories from *Black Misery* (1969) and *The Pasteboard Bandit* (1935; 1997). Rounding out the children's literary world are five juvenile histories by Hughes: *The First Book of Negroes* (1952), *The First Book of Rhythms* (1954), *The First Book of Jazz* (1955), *The First Book of the West Indies* (1956), and *The First Book of Africa* (1960). Especially for those of us who often prioritize the poetry—while wondering exactly what the author was doing between *Montage of a Dream Deferred* (1951) and *Ask Your Mama* (1961)—his juvenilia and stories account for sustained work during the decade.

Since the centennial of Hughes's birth in 2002, a resurgence of his reputation continues. In June of that year, bolstered by leadership of the NAACP in Cleveland, the Case Western Historical Society commenced a yearlong celebration of the poet's life and work. California State University at Dominguez Hills and Yale University commissioned conferences to celebrate the legacy. Lawrence, Kansas, the residential city of Hughes's grandmother, hosted a definitive conference directed by Maryemma Graham and John Edgar Tidwell. In addition to the usual academic crowds (see Tracy, A *Historical Guide to Langston Hughes* 2004), many laypersons participated.

About then, Beverly Jarrett, editor in chief of the University of Missouri Press, pointed me toward a focus for the *Collected Works*, volume 15, on short stories by Langston Hughes. Arnold Rampersad chaired the editorial board that facilitated publication of the *Works* as a whole. Steven C. Tracy, in A *Historical Guide to Langston Hughes* (Oxford 2004), provided a polished outlet for honing insights developed during the editorial work for the University of Missouri Press. The International Conference on Narrative Theory, Nice, France, 1991, and the Third International Conference on New Directions, University of Cambridge, United Kingdom, 2005, facilitated forums for articulating a global theory so encapsulated within Hughes's stories. To all, I am indebted.

R. Baxter Miller
Athens, Georgia

WORKS CITED

Harper, Donna Akiba Sullivan. *Not So Simple: The "Simple" Stories by Langston Hughes.* Columbia: University of Missouri Press, 1995.

Hughes, Langston. *The Collected Poems of Langston Hughes.* Edited by Arnold Rampersad, with the assistance of David Roessel. New York: Knopf, 1994.

———. *The Collected Works of Langston Hughes.* 16 vols. Columbia: University of Missouri Press, 2001–.

———. *Langston Hughes and the* Chicago Defender: *Essays on Race, Politics, and Culture, 1942–62.* Edited by Christopher C. De Santis. Urbana: University of Illinois Press, 1995.

———. *The Political Plays of Langston Hughes.* With introductions and analyses by Susan Duffy. Carbondale: Southern Illinois University Press, 2000.

——. *Short Stories*. Edited by Akiba Sullivan Harper. New York: Hill and Wang, 1996.

——. *Works for Children and Young Adults: Poetry, Fiction, and Other Writing.* Edited by Dianne Johnson. Vol. 11, *The Collected Works of Langston Hughes.* Columbia: University of Missouri Press, 2003.

——, and Carl Van Vechten. *Remember Me to Harlem: The Letters of Langston Hughes and Carl Van Vechten, 1925–1964.* Edited by Emily Bernard. New York: Knopf, 2001.

McLaren, Joseph. "Langston Hughes and Africa: From the Harlem Renaissance to the 1960s." In *Juxtapositions: The Harlem Renaissance and the Lost Generation,* edited by Lesley Marx, Loes Nas, and Chandré Carstens, 77–94. Cape Town, South Africa: University of Cape Town, 2000.

——. *Langston Hughes, Folk Dramatist in the Protest Tradition, 1921–1943.* Contributions in Afro-American and African Studies 181. Westport, Conn: Greenwood Press, 1997.

Miller, R. Baxter. "Café de la paix: Mapping the Harlem Renaissance." *South Atlantic Review* 65, no. 2 (2000): 73–94.

——. "Framing and Framed Languages in Hughes's *Ask Your Mama: 12 Moods for Jazz.*" *MELUS* 17, no. 4 (1991–1992): 3–13.

——. "Langston Hughes, 1902–1967." In *A Historical Guide to Langston Hughes,* edited by Steven C. Tracy, 23–62. New York: Oxford University Press, 2004.

——. "Reinvention and Globalization in Hughes's Stories." *MELUS* 30, no. 1 (2005): 69–83.

Ostrom, Hans A. *Langston Hughes: A Study of the Short Fiction.* Twayne's Studies in Short Fiction, 47. New York: Twayne, 1993.

Roessel, David. "'A Racial Act': The Letters of Langston Hughes and Ezra Pound." *Paideuma: A Journal Devoted to Ezra Pound Scholarship* 29, no. 1–2 (2000): 207–42.

Tracy, Steven C. Introduction to *A Historical Guide to Langston Hughes,* 3–22. New York: Oxford University Press, 2004.

Trotman, C. James, ed. *Langston Hughes: The Man, His Art, and His Continuing Influence.* Garland Reference Library of the Humanities, 1872; Critical Studies in Black Life and Culture, 29. New York: Garland, 1995.

Woods, Gregory. "Gay Re-Readings of the Harlem Renaissance Poets." In *Critical Essays: Gay and Lesbian Writers of Color,* edited by Emmanuel S. Nelson, 127–42. New York: Haworth, 1993.

INTRODUCTION

What Langston Hughes experienced in Paris on New Year's Eve in 1937 revealed the most telling patterns in his literary imagination. Having gone to an opera, he had planned to catch up with some friends of Leon Damas, the French Guiana poet and protégé of André Gide, and proceed to a party in the Latin Quarter. On his way down stairs to the Metro, however, he found that he had left the address for the party back at his hotel, so he turned instead down the nearly deserted streets leading toward the Madeleine. Carefully he watched the approach of a slightly limping man, head pulled down in his overcoat and collar raised against the cold. It was Seki Sano, an old friend and director of Japanese theater. The two men entered the glass enclosure of a sidewalk cafe, empty except for a pretty woman setting alone at another table.

As the artists looked out on the lonely boulevard, Sano offered consolation and regret for Hughes' expulsion from Japan in 1933 and said that he himself was also exiled. When the waiter lightened the gloom by exclaiming "Bonne Année," Hughes and Sano lifted their glasses as the bells tolled in 1938. The woman began suddenly to cry. Invited to join them, she sat quietly at their table, struggling to hold back tears, until the bells became silent. Then she thanked the men, said good night, and disappeared down the boulevard toward the Madeleine. Sano and Hughes shook hands at the corner across from the Café de la Paix and parted. Sano headed for the Left Bank and Hughes for Montmartre. Passing the Galleries Lafayette and the Gare Saint Lazare, the poet turned to climb a slight incline.

Where would I be when the next New Year came, I wondered? By then, would there be war—a major war? Would
Mussolini and Hitler have finished their practice in Ethiopia
and Spain to turn their planes on the rest of us? Would
civilization be destroyed? Would the world really end?
    "Not my world," I said to myself. "My world will not
end."
    But worlds—entire nations and civilizations—do end.
In the snowy night in the shadows of the old houses of
Montmartre, I repeated to myself, "My world won't end."
    But how could I be so sure? I don't know.
    For a moment I wondered.[1]

> In one hand
> I hold tragedy
> And in the other
> Comedy—
> Masks for the Soul.
> —Langston Hughes, "Jester"

Here are the deep tropes in his literary world, for the quest for
meaning fills the void between tragic time and the fraternal release from it. Tragedy marks the passing of years and the desertion
of friends. Where all would seem lost to loneliness and impending
war, friends have drunk in the festive mood and celebrated the
New Year. Whatever the different roads lying ahead of them,
they carry a sense of comradeliness out into the figurative night.
    For the purposes of this study, literary imagination means the
tropes and rhetorical vehicles through which Langston Hughes
imparted human meaning to his readers. It means the process by
which he mediated between social limitation and the dream of
freedom.[2] The conception derives only in part from the Enlightenment as far back as in 1780: "the understanding of genius,
poetic power, and originality or sympathy, individuality, knowledge, and even of ethics." To Hughes, the imagination recon-
ciled and identified "man with nature, the subjective with the
objective, the internal mind with the external world, time with

eternity, matter with spirit, the finite with the infinite, the conscious with the unconscious, and the self-consciousness with the
absence of self-consciousness." It related "the static to the dynamic, the passive to the active, the ideal to the real, and the
universal to the particular."[3]

While Hughes avoided the aristocratic and exalted tone of
British romanticism, he represented the poet as the voice of
beauty and wisdom. He achieved metonyms that disclosed either
harmony with nature or the self's divorce from nature. For
Hughes, as for Coleridge—though a great cultural chasm divides
the two—imagination was not an act of memory or fancy; it was
the ordering power that defined itself in its own light. While the
imaginative process involved the retention of old ideas, it meant
the constant reworking of them.[4]

This book reconsiders the complex patterns of meaning in the
literary imagination of Langston Hughes, especially as they complement and displace each other, including the genres that contain them and the creative strategies that set them into play. I
inquire into the voice and signature of the man as well as the
narrator in his literary world. It is possible to look first to the
historical and biographical sources, then to the autobiographical
imagination. Next the discussion turns to the centrality of Black
woman in such poems as "Mother to Son" and "Madam and the
Fortune Teller." Poems of this kind are keys to understanding
the rise and decline of Hughes' creativity, the process leading
finally to some swings between tragedy and comedy. What follows
includes a close reading of the lyrical imagination that ranks
Hughes as perhaps the foremost Black American poet of the kind:
he restored lyricism to a rite of cultural celebration.

The figurative quality permits the lyric in autobiography and
the lyric poem to suspend the tragic time (history and death)
that, outside of people, threatens the world within them or even
the aesthetic world itself. An equal skill in metaphor enables the
poems on women to achieve a great emotional range, and the
effort strengthens the hopeful tone in many of the political
poems. Even when Langston Hughes seemed almost to cry at Jim

Crow discrimination, he had to laugh at it as well, for humor empowered his capacity to endure and prevail over ill. So it is that tragicomedy subsumed his spirit and nearly all his literary forms as well. Indeed, the mode was the hidden unity behind his choice of genres and his fertile imagination. The ideas appear in a different order now from that in which I first wrote them down. I had written about the poems on women and the short fiction during the mid-1970s before a critical reading of *I Wonder as I Wander* enabled me to decode the unities and metaphors throughout Hughes' work. From the vantage point of this second autobiography, I retraced my interpretations in the earlier essays and then went on to chart new ground about Hughes' lyrical imagination as public performance. Everything led to and away from the artistic strategies of the political imagination. I had learned particularly to appreciate the way that Hughes transcended the boundaries of public and private art.

Now the critical method is eclectic, the emphasis being on the way that myth reveals itself through genre and history. The political poems lend themselves to a Freudian analysis insofar as they disclose the questionability of unconscionable power. Whatever the occasional need for psychological criticism, it is obvious that a phenomenological approach works well for the study of Hughes. Often his voice suggests not only the Harlem Renaissance in particular or the United States in general but modernity itself. Hughes, already a mature adult in the atomic age, retreated inwardly from the image of "Daybreak in Alabama" (1940) to an awareness of the mushroom cloud ("Junior Addict," 1967). It is obvious now that the contemporary terror that threatened his imagination—what would today invoke the terminology of postmodernism—subsequently informed the poetic worlds of Philip Larkin, Ted Hughes, Robert Lowell, and Gwendolyn Brooks. While many scholars have documented the significance of the time and culture for Hughes, I have tried to read the pattern by which a Black American Dream seeks to redeem itself from historical time.

Though the study tends to move in fresh directions, it can do so only by taking into account the standard contributions to Hughes scholarship. For bibliographical consultation, it depends most heavily on research by Donald C. Dickinson and Therman B. O'Daniel during the 1960s and 1970s.[5] Since the pioneering work by James A. Emanuel in 1967, a handful of works by scholars such as Faith Berry, Richard K. Barksdale, and Arnold Rampersad have solidified the historical as well as the biographical context for Hughes study in recent years.[6] Regarding Hughes' importance to the African diaspora, works by Lemuel Johnson, Edward J. Mullen, and Martha Cobb spanned across the 1970s.[7] For a broad look at Hughes in the context of cultural studies, *Opportunity* was a particularly valuable journal in the 1920s as *Phylon* would be in the 1940s and 1950s. Near the time of Hughes' death in 1967, the *CLA Journal*, *Freedomways*, *Crisis*, and *Présence Africaine* all brought out special issues worthy of scholarly consideration.

This book advances the previous scholarship because it explores the properties of genre and the imaginative re-creation of history through the creative work itself. To clarify the interplay of motifs, I replace themes within the structure of the works and the larger *oeuvre*. Hughes appears here as a narrative self as well as an ironist and moralist. Though he was a social and political rebel, he was an early deconstructionist as well: he subverted the very conventions of genre through which tradition and modernity have sought to confine the free imagination. He was "scornful in subject matter, in photography, and rhythmical treatment [and I would add theory as well as form] of whatever obstructions time and tradition . . . placed before him."[8]

Though earlier studies have focused on either the informative or the rudimentary description of theme, on historical accounts, or on helpful introductions to the poetry, my approach here assumes a more philosophical audience. The interest is equally in the artistic struggle for literary forms, especially as they reveal the writer's personal and social dream, and in the appreciation of Black American culture. But my aim is to achieve a sophistication of inquiry without resorting to a cliquish jargon that might obscure sensitive appreciation. In addressing those readers who are interested in literary theory, as well as in applying practical criticism to the texts, I attempt to reassess the artistic accomplishments and the critical ground they rest upon. Langston Hughes, whether in "The Negro Speaks of Rivers" (1921), *The Big Sea* (1940), *One-Way Ticket* (1949), or *The Panther and the Lash* (1967), emerges as a writer whose complex use of metaphor belied his seemingly transparent treatment of folk life. Though he certainly earned his claim to the title of "People's Poet"—for he was indeed one of the most loved and accessible of all American authors—his writings merit a far closer examination. Even the ablest scholars have ignored the secrets of his practice and theory.

The explicated texts, selected for their own aesthetic merit and representative theme, also demonstrate the connection between appreciation and theory. They appear sequentially here as they do within the published volumes that best represent his experimentation in the particular genres under discussion. Hughes produced two autobiographies, nearly a score of volumes and pamphlets of poetry, and ten books of "fiction" (depending on our label for the "Simple" sketches) during his lifetime; at least eleven plays were in production between 1935 and 1963.[9] (The novels and dramas are not detailed, but the present book helps at least to clarify the tragicomic principles pervading the dramatic scenes of Hughes' literary performers.) Though the selections may appear at times to have been chosen at random, they represent carefully the various stages—early, middle, and late—across the forty-six years of the author's literary career. Hence, we maintain a sense of Hughes' own imaginative ordering of the poems in the works published in book form.

Given the impossibility of dealing with the enormous opus of short fiction (Twayne Publishers recently proposed a contract on that topic alone), I have chosen for explication several stories—"Father and Son," "Shadow of the Blues," and "Lynn Clarisse"—that exemplify the complex range of Hughes' literary imagination, for therein can be seen, respectively, the mythic type of profound alienation derived from his own personal life with his father, James Nathaniel Hughes, as well as from Black American history; the artistic redemption of blues as both confrontation with and transcendence over brutal social murder and discrimination; and the awareness that even the Black man of literary imagination must finally still live in history. The purpose, in other words, is to recover the spiritual strivings of the Black masses engaged in the reshaping of American vision.

1

"FOR A MOMENT I WONDERED"
The Autobiographical Imagination

In his *Soliloquy on Viewing My Life*, W.E.B. Du Bois writes brilliantly about the verbal form that fuses myth and history.

Autobiographies do not form indisputable authorities. They are always incomplete, and often unreliable. Eager as I am to put down the truth, there are difficulties; memory fails, especially in small details, so that it becomes finally but a theory of my life, with much forgotten and misconceived, with valuable testimony but often less than absolutely true. . . . Prejudiced I certainly am by my twisted life; by the way in which I have been treated by my fellows, by what I myself have thought and done. . . . What I think of myself, now and in the past, furnishes no certain document proving what I really am. Mostly my life today is a mass of memories with vast omissions, matters which are forgotten accidentally or by deep design. . . . One must then see these varying views [as distinct from the previous versions] in contradictions to truth, and not as final and complete authority. This book then is the Soliloquy of an old man on what he dreams his life has been as he sees it slowly drifting away; and what he would like others to believe.[1]

The statement suggests the principles necessary to explain the autobiographies of Langston Hughes. While fact has occurred quantitatively, truth is qualitative. Fact means measurement according to scientific history, but truth implies an almost religious certainty. Truth is the spiritual interpretation of fact through self. While the autobiographer's memory documents and recalls events from the personal life or the historical source, it imposes a personal fiction or imagined belief upon them. Memory creates, in other words, a complex of symbolic actions defined here as myth.

For Langston Hughes, who held suspect the merely philosophical and detached, the proposition about myth and meaning would hardly be worthwhile. Nor does it apply to residual formalists Cleanth Brooks and W.K. Wimsatt, who warn against the intentional fallacy. Perhaps the latter would doubt the wisdom of elevating autobiography to literary art. But the structure in *The Big Sea* (1940) and *I Wonder As I Wander* (1956) reveals a theory of the performed arts and an imaginative revision of literary as well as historical sources. The narrative self identifies with both the literally and the figuratively dramatic performers he encounters yet continues to travel through Harlem, Paris, and Madrid. While the speaker narrates the story of his autobiographical self clearly, or of himself as a past traveler plainly, he understands the roles of the figurative dramatist and singer as well. It may prove enlightening to test whether Langston Hughes enacts and reenacts the ritualistic engagement with literary sources and relations and to inquire whether he suggests elsewhere the ritualistic performance of song that demonstrates human communion between the performing singer and the listener.

These autobiographies are not only the kind of narrative discourse that orders historical experience. Their prose conceals lyrics that seem almost to arrest the adolescent pains carried over from childhood or the imminent destruction of World War II. To Hughes, autobiography is often literary history, not the mythic pattern through which the narrator creates a mirror image

of himself. At times he projects himself into the mask of the
dramatist, writer, and singer, for as artistic creators, at least, they
are the same. What I want to consider most strongly is the way
that his narrator's symbiotic bond with other emblems of interpretation and history reveals a common thread of cultural immortality or aesthetic preservation, yet a profound paradox as
well and a holistic conception of time.

Rarely observed by scholars, his double impulse toward myth
and history had appeared clearly in the opening paragraph of the
short story "Home (originally published in *Esquire*):" "When the
boy came back, there were bright stickers and tags in strange
languages the home folks couldn't read all over his bags, and on
his violin far-away borders, big hotels in European cities, and
steamers that crossed the ocean a long way from Hopkinsville.
They made the leather-colored bags and black violin case look
very gay and circus-like. They made white people on the train
wonder [my emphasis] about the brown-skinned young man to
whom the baggage belonged. And when he got off at a village
station in Missouri, the loafers gathered around in a crowd, star-
ing."[2] Here white travelers "wonder" about Roy Williams, the
violinist and jazz player, who "wandered" around the world. To
Langston Hughes, even then, "wander" referred to the world of
historical narrative, but "wonder" implied lyrical interpretation.
The distinction is crucial to many other antitheses, including
those of fact and truth, fact and fiction, materiality and imma-
teriality, history and reflection, dynamic time and inert timelessness.

Sometimes the narrator mediates adeptly between competing
worlds. To Hughes, the narrative conceals lyric moments that
freeze its order temporarily and imprint the design of the authorial
self on history. From the Harlem Renaissance in 1925 through
the Great Depression in 1934, linear history moves forward in
the texts to the Spanish Civil War in 1937. Yet mythic history—
the spirit or pattern connecting them—challenges the very conception of sequential order.

However attractive the compulsion to explicate both autobiographies in detail, it will suffice to analyze the way in which the dialectical tension between autobiographical imagination and history pervades them. Through arrestments or lyric freezes, the work sometimes preserves personalities and events better than it reveals the autobiographical self (1910-21); it expresses doubt that Hughes' imagination can even imprint an interpretive order upon the Harlem Renaissance (1922-31); and it shows an imaginative as well as engaged self only periodically (1932-38). Though the process of narrative engagement means the autobiographer's identification with the people and events experienced, interpretation suggests a complementary strategy of analysis and evaluation.

In *The Big Sea* Langston Hughes reminisces about the second summer vacation of his high school years: "I never will forget the thrill of first understanding the French of de Maupassant. The soft snow was falling through one of his stories in the little book we used in school, and that I had worked over so long, before I really felt the snow falling there. Then all of a sudden one night the beauty and the meaning of the words in which he made the snow fall, came to me. I think it was de Maupassant who made me really want to be a writer and write stories about Negroes, so true that people in far-away lands would read them— even after I was dead" (*BS*, 33-34). These words are striking because they show Hughes intuitively grasping the principle of negritude—the ethnic or cultural base that one can expand to universality. He would seek to do for Black Americans what Maupassant had done for nineteenth-century France: to immortalize the culture and perceptions of a nation or race.

Langston Hughes' works preserve the jazz rhythms of his time, the southern dialect with which he was familiar, and both the pathos and humor of the folk Blacks whom he loved. Yet what does one say about *The Big Sea*? Although it often appears on reading lists for Afro-American literature and culture, critics have generally ignored it. In the *Saturday Review* (31 August 1940, p. 12) Oswald Villard called the book "a most valuable contribution to the struggle of the Negro for life and justice and freedom and

intellectual liberty in America." Donald C. Dickinson, one of
Hughes' biographers, adds: "*The Big Sea* is valuable not only as
the story of a man's life but as a candid look at an era which
according to Richard Wright [*New Republic*, 28 October 1940,
p. 600] Hughes analyzed with 'humor, urbanity and objectivi-
ty.' "3

The Big Sea preserves a history of events often better than it
sustains a metaphor of the creative self. Yet listing the dates of
Hughes' plays or of his school days necessitates much looking
backward and forward in the text. Even after locating a date,
one cannot be sure it is always the right one: did Bert Williams
really die in 1921? Since transitions are wanting, one must be
skeptical. Chronological histories tell us correctly that Williams
died in 1922. Though Hughes probably knows that the year
changes during his narration, he does not tell us so. He often
gives historical fact but has his own loose and confusing mode
of presentation. Because the result bewilders critics, Dickinson
says that *The Big Sea* ends in 1929. Actually the history in the
work stretches from Hughes' birth in 1902 to the death of A'Lelia
Walker in 1931 and the Scottsboro case of the same year.

Just as *The Big Sea* reminds us of literary history, it reminds
us of the western movement that characterized the United States
in the 1800s and ended in the 1890s. One of Hughes' experiences
as a child suggests the urbanization of what had once been the
new promised land. At fourteen, living with his Auntee Reed,
whose house is near a depot, he walks down to the Sante Fe
Station, stares at the railroad tracks—and dreams about Chicago.
The frontier is over; from Kansas he looks northeast to the city,
not southwest toward Santa Fe, because "civilization" has sup-
planted western promise.

His movement to Lincoln, Illinois, in 1916 is an example of
the great migration of that decade, when Blacks were pulling up
roots in the South and journeying north in hope of better jobs
and better pay. His family becomes a symbol of all the restless
and wandering Blacks then. With his mother and stepfather
Hughes moves again, this time to Cleveland, where his stepfather

retires from the steel mill to become a janitor. These scenes preserve for the future a vision of American industry during the period. The crowded working conditions, the difficulty of finding a place to live, the expensive rents—all these characterize the time that *The Big Sea* records.

The work preserves not only the social realities of its time but the contemporary literature. At Central High in Cleveland, Ethel Weimer, teacher of English, introduces Hughes to the work of Carl Sandburg, Amy Lowell, Vachel Lindsay, and Edgar Lee Masters. Sandburg is particularly significant because he, like Hughes, belongs in the Walt Whitman tradition.[4] Viewing literary figures through *The Big Sea* allows the reader to experience time multidimensionally and to see the new poetry movement of 1912 through the eyes of Hughes the narrator, who becomes twenty-one in 1923.

The past that Hughes preserves shows racial discrimination, especially toward the end of World War I: "I soon realized that the kikes and the spicks and the hunkies—scorned though they might be by the pure Americans—all had it on the niggers in one thing. Summer time came and they could get jobs quickly" (*BS*, 32). At the close of the war, Hughes realizes the paradox of the American Dream, which rewards whites but punishes Blacks. The idea would enrich much of his verse and prose: "Theaters and restaurants in the downtown area began to refuse to accommodate colored people. Landlords doubled and tripled the rents at the approach of a dark tenant. And when the white soldiers came back from the war, Negroes were often discharged from their jobs and white men hired in their places" (*BS*, 51).

Hughes' year at Columbia University parallels the opening of *Shuffle Along*, the popular show that began its long run in the Music Hall on 63rd Street in New York City on May 23, 1921. Hughes, watching Florence Mills perform in the star role, sat in the audience night after night.[5] While the experience did not help to distinguish his performance at the university, the opportunity did advance his initiation into the appreciation of Black art forms.

In *The Big Sea* one finds the paradox of both white and Black America during these 1920s. Especially vivid and biting is the portrait of the Black middle class in Washington, whose members maintain the rigid lines of class and color within the race. The irony is that these Blacks accept and mirror the absurd values of the American mainstream, which segregates Blacks even as it praises their exoticism and primitivism. Too often the autobiographical self of *The Big Sea* withdraws and refuses to judge, but not here: "The 'better class' Washington colored people . . . were on the whole as unbearable and snobbish a group of people as I have ever come in contact with anywhere. They lived in comfortable homes, had fine cars, played bridge, drank Scotch, gave exclusive 'formal' parties and dressed well, but seemed to me altogether lacking in real culture, kindness, and good common sense" (*BS*, 206-7).

The book records a world in which Black snobbishness coexists with Black art: one woman calls Hughes' mother Carrie on the phone to warn her not to attend a formal dinner honoring the "New Negro" because Carrie, the woman says, probably lacks an evening gown. At social gatherings, members of this class boast about being descendants of the best Southern white families. Ironically, they hate themselves and love white society. Hughes criticizes the Jim Crowism of 1924: "I could not get a cup of coffee on a cold day anywhere within sight of the Capitol, because no 'white' restaurant would serve a Negro. I could not see the new motion pictures, because they did not play in the Negro houses" (*BS*, 206).

Where Hughes creates a permanent vision of a past, personal doubt shadows the artistic achievement of the age. Roland Hayes filling up Carnegie Hall with listeners, Paul Robeson drawing crowds in London, and Florence Mills performing on two continents inspire a detached admiration. So do the Rose McClendon Players, Bessie Smith, and Josephine Baker at Harlem's Cotton Club. Almost in the same breath, Hughes, who often treats his narration as if it were someone else's, interrupts: "But I was never there, because the Cotton Club was a Jim Crow club for gangsters and affluent whites. They were not cordial to Negro patronage, unless you were a celebrity like Bojangles" (BS, 224). Understanding the paradox of a white society that flocks to see Black artists but restricts Blacks from viewing these same artists, Hughes indeed recognized the irony. Whatever small unity we find in *The Big Sea* comes in the connection between the foregoing passage and this section's ending: "I was there [when the Negro was in vogue]. I had a swell time while it lasted. But I thought it wouldn't last long. . . . For how could a large and enthusiastic number of people be crazy about Negroes forever? . . . The ordinary Negroes hadn't heard of the Negro Renaissance. And if they had, it hadn't raised their wages any" (BS, 228).

In the last seventy-seven pages especially, Hughes preserves the different tones of the Renaissance: humor, sadness, and irony. For a Harlem audience, Jules Bledsoe is comic when acting the role of Brutus in Eugene O'Neill's *Emperor Jones*. Harlemites laugh at seeing this naked Black fleeing across a stage, even if Little Frightened Fears are supposed to be pursuing him. The reviews of his own *Fine Clothes to the Jew* (1927), moreover, sadden Hughes because most of its hostile critics are Black—commentators who assumed that self-denial, an abandoning of dialect and sexual imagery, would lead to acceptance in white society.

Because the chronology of *The Big Sea* is bewildering, the reader interested merely in historical fact should look elsewhere. David Levering Lewis, *When Harlem Was in Vogue*; Nathan Huggins, *Harlem Renaissance*; James Weldon Johnson, *Black Manhattan*; Arna Bontemps, *The Harlem Renaissance Remembered*; John Hope Franklin, *From Slavery to Freedom*; Lerone Bennett, Jr., *Before the Mayflower*, all provide more accurate accounts. But we shall lose something in such an exchange, for *The Big Sea* preserves more than dates; it records colorful biography, the important people of an important time.

The men and women whom Hughes portrays could form a "Who Was Who in Black America." "Nash" or George Walker, a famous Black comedian, came from Hughes' hometown of Law-rence, Kansas. Once Walker played his phonograph there for the benefit of the church's mortgage fund. Six years later Hughes attends the funeral of Bert Williams, Walker's partner, in New York, just as he had attended Walker's in Kansas. The related occurrences are striking not because the members of this comedy team died at different times, not because their achievements span the end of one century and the beginning of the next, but because the narrative Hughes lives in the text as well. This frozen self withstands time, even though the real Hughes died in 1967.

The Big Sea freezes other personages too outside of time. One is Florence Mills, a star of the Renaissance. Another is Alain Locke, a Rhodes Scholar, Ph.D., and professor of philosophy at Howard University. A third is Jessie Fauset, managing editor of The *Crisis*, who invites Hughes to a luncheon. Here, in 1923, Marcus Garvey still appears at the height of his power; he died in 1940, the very year in which *The Big Sea* came out. In each instance, Hughes shifts to the encountered figures the quality of creative energy normally reserved for the autobiographical self, making them only more objective extensions of his own most timeless voice.

After Cullen tells Hughes about a cabaret party and benefit for the National Association for the Advancement of Colored People, Hughes attends and meets many leading figures of the day: Walter White, an executive of the NAACP; Mary White Ovington, author of *Portraits in Color*; James Weldon Johnson, author of *Black Manhattan*; and Carl Van Vechten, author of *Nigger Heaven*. In contrast, one sees Carter G. Woodson, director of the Association for the Study of Negro Life and History, only in outline; the same is true of Aaron Douglas, a famous painter of the period. Hughes immortalizes a select group and its deeds. Here, however, is not only the portraiture but the symbiotic bond between them as significant determiners in Black American his-tory and himself as the reimaginer of it. "Jessie Fauset at the *Crisis*, Charles Johnson at *Opportunity*, and Alain Locke in Wash-ington, were the three people who midwifed the so-called New

Negro literature into being. Kind and critical—but not too critical for the young—they nursed us along until our books were
born. Countee Cullen, Zora Neale Hurston, Arna Bontemps,
Rudolph Fisher, Wallace Thurman, Jean Toomer, Nella Larsen,
all of us came along about the same time. Most of us are quite
grown up now. Some are silent. Some are dead" (BS, 218). The
irony, of course, is that the only ones who are dead in terms of
The Big Sea are those whom the book does not portray and, hence,
immortalize.

The images of Gladys Bentley and Wallace Thurman still endure well. Bentley appears as two personalities, one before and
one after the fall from innocence into commercialism. First the
singer is "a large, dark masculine lady, whose feet pounded the
floor while her fingers pounded the keyboard—a perfect piece
of African sculpture animated by her own rhythm" (BS, 226).
Later, she acquires an accompanist, moves downtown, and writes
in Hollywood—she becomes a star.

The depiction of Wallace Thurman is even more striking,
perhaps because, as Patricia E. Taylor asserts, Hughes admires
him the most.[6] But an ambivalence undermines this admiration
partially because Hughes portrays Thurman as as "a strangely
brilliant black boy, who had read everything, and whose critical
mind could find something wrong with everything he read" (BS,
234). At parties Thurman threatened to jump out of windows;
at other times he was a ghost writer for True Story. Nowhere else
in The Big Sea does Hughes strike this brilliance of character-
ization: "He [Thurman] was a strange kind of fellow, who liked
to drink gin, but didn't like to drink gin; who liked being a Negro,
but felt it a great handicap; who adored bohemianism, but
thought it wrong to be a bohemian. He liked to waste a lot of
time, but he always felt guilty wasting time. He loathed crowds,
yet he hated to be alone. He almost always felt bad, yet he didn't
write poetry" (BS, 238). Hughes presents Thurman who is pes-
simistic about the future of Black American literature, one who
thinks that the easiness of the Renaissance has spoiled those
involved and made them undisciplined.

The reader gets some vision also of Jean Toomer, who marries Margery Latimer, a white novelist, and who insists to newspapers that he is no more colored than white. The reader learns, too, the Toomer refused to contribute poems to James Weldon Johnson's *Book of Negro Poetry* because he saw himself by then as having transcended race into the universal.

Of the remaining personages, Hughes preserves most concretely Zora Hurston, Rudolph Fisher, and A'Lelia Walker. To many whites, Hurston was a "perfect 'darkie,' in the nice meaning they give the term—that is a naive, childlike, sweet, humorous, and highly colored Negro" (BS, 239). As a young medical student, he is a rounded character, if not as intriguing or influential in the text as Locke or Thurman. Fisher writes stories for *Atlantic Monthly* and wisecracks with Alain Locke, as Hughes looks on in quiet admiration. During his college days Fisher had sung with Paul Robeson, and like Wallace Thurman he died in December 1934. Portrayed in the text as being both dead and alive, Robeson and Thurman are forever being reborn there.

The image of A'Lelia Walker is equally eternal. This "gorgeous dark Amazon" has a townhouse in New York and a country mansion on the Hudson. That her mother made a great fortune from hair straightening suggests another paradox: we find A'Lelia immortalized as the party patron of the period, yet the money she spends to entertain the bohemian artists who seek Black identity comes, ironically, from this process of racial acculturation. Nevertheless, A'Lelia remains the "joy-goddess" of Harlem's 1920s (BS, 245).

The portrait of Mary McLeod Bethune, one of the most important educators of the period, reveals the same paradox: At A'Lelia's funeral she praises this dead woman's mother for bringing "the gift of beauty to Negro womanhood" (BS, 246). What shows the irony of the Renaissance better than this? A eulogy for A'Lelia, who so often entertained the New Negro, becomes praise for her mother, who furthered the cause of racial assimilation. In complementing *The Big Sea* with a reading of *I Wonder as I Wander* and Dickinson's *Bio-Bibliography*, one gets a more

complete impression of the real Bethune. With Hughes she traveled often and laughed; once, when he read "The Negro Mother," she wept.[7]

> Children, I come back today
> To tell you a story of the long dark way
> That I had to climb, that I had to know
> . . . .
> Oh, my dark children, may my dreams and my prayers
> Impel you forever up the great stairs.[8]

But the Bethune portrayed in *The Big Sea* must play and replay
another role. At the end of the Harlem Renaissance she illustrates
the paradox of Black American identity.

The Big Sea leaves similarly incomplete its sketches of Arna
Bontemps and Carl Van Vechten. The first exists as something
of a mystery. Quiet and scholarly, like the young Du Bois, he
hides the wife who is always having golden babies. Van Vechten's
indirect portrait is a propagandistic eulogy more than a realistic
description, and regarding him, more than anyone else, Hughes
is naive.[9]

> For several pleasant years, he gave an annual birthday party
> for James Weldon Johnson, young Alfred A. Knopf, Jr.,
> and himself, for their birthdays fall on the same day. At
> the last of these parties the year before Mr. Johnson died,
> on the Van Vechten table there were three cakes, one red,
> one white, and one blue—the colors of our flag. They ho-
> nored a Gentile, a Negro, and a Jew—friends and fellow
> Americans. But the differences of race did not occur to me
> until days later, when I thought back about the three colors
> and the three men. Carl Van Vechten is like that party.
> He never talks grandiloquently about democracy or Ameri-
> canism. Nor makes a fetish of those qualities. But he lives
> them with sincerity—and humor.   [BS 254-55]

Like Hughes' patron Charlotte Mason (unnamed in the book),
Van Vechten actually has a fascination for the primitive. Why

else would he allow a woman with a gun to stand outside his door, waiting to kill her husband? "At another party of his (but this was incidental) the guests were kept in a constant state of frightful expectancy by a lady standing in the hall outside Mr. Van Vechten's door, who announced that she was waiting for her husband to emerge from the opposite apartment, where he was visiting another woman. When I came to the party, I saw her standing grimly there. . . . And she displayed to Mrs. Van Vechten's maids the pistol in her handbag" (BS, 253).

The Big Sea portrays Wallace Thurman and Zora Hurston more completely than it does Langston Hughes, for it creates a detached self, a Hughes that belongs in successful fiction rather than the engaged self that should characterize skillful autobiography. This is a significant distinction, for the first self subordinates its identity to the observation of others and to the dramatic situations encountered; the second self, on the contrary, interprets both events and persons. True autobiography is historical fact as an imaginative mind responds to it and as the mind organizes a comprehensive moral vision. Memoir, however, is less a process of this human action and awareness than a writer's objective record of his times. The Life and Times of Frederick Douglass and Autobiography of Malcolm X are autobiographies; The Big Sea is a memoir.

It would be an oversimplification, however, to say with George E. Kent that Hughes wrote two autobiographies without revealing himself.[10] Because Hughes does expose himself partly in The Big Sea and I Wonder as I Wander, the distinction made in the paragraph above is more accurate. Nevertheless, though we catch rare glimpses of Hughes the man, this narrator does withdraw often into obscurity and silence, leaving the reader to make his or her own sense of social or historical disorder. The Big Sea presents the Hughes who responds to minor events but fails to record clearly the Hughes who reacts to personal crises. We know that he is hurt when the Africans look at him and fail to find him Black, or when a teacher in Topeka talks about his race in order to embarrass him. Even then, however, we discover

Hughes' love for humanity. Other students attack him after hear-
ing this teacher's cruel words, yet he remembers one white boy
who always took up for him and others who sometimes did. "I
learned early not to hate *all* white people. And ever since, it has
seemed to me that *most* people are generally good . . . in every
country where I have been" (*BS*, 14). The Hughes of *The Big
Sea* never comes to doubt this dictum completely. But bound by
the frozen time of his created world there, he never ages beyond
twenty-nine or thirty. In 1967, Hughes would have to reaffirm
this hopeful vision through the narrator of "Daybreak in Alabama"—the poem, reprinted from *Unquote* (1940), that ends
The Panther and the Lash—for by then the real Hughes would
have lived through a nightmare of cynicism and disbelief.

So Hughes the man and Hughes the fictional creation go their
separate ways: in *The Big Sea* the latter remains often tolerant,
concerned, and sympathetic. After his grandmother's death
Hughes goes to live with Auntee Reed and her husband. She is
a Christian who makes the boy go to church every Sunday, and
he is a sinner who washes overalls in a big iron pot in the back-
yard, "but both of them were very good and kind—the one who
went to church and the one who didn't. And no doubt from
them I learned to like both Christians and sinners equally well"
(*BS*, 18). Sometimes it is difficult to find this tolerant and sympathetic narrator, because the chronology jumps back and forth
so much. Going with his mother to Lincoln, Illinois, at fourteen,
Hughes recalls being six, his age when in Topeka, Kansas, she
introduced him to the library. A triple sense of time results in
this scene as we listen to the narration by Hughes the man.
Because *The Big Sea* begins *in medias res*, with an incident that
occurred when the author was twenty-one, this passage reinforces
the jumbled sense of time that characterizes the beginning: "Even
before I was six [present age fourteen], books began to happen
to me, so that after a while, there came a time when I believed
in books more than in people—which, of course, was wrong.
That was why, when I went to Africa [age twenty-one], I threw
all the books into the sea" (*BS*, 26).

The Big Sea preserves an image of a Hughes who participates in many events and who becomes enlightened. For two years he is on a track team that wins two citywide championships. He is a lieutenant in the military training corps. He edits the yearbook for his high school class of 1920. He learns about discipline and the possibility of changing values: from Miss Dieke, his art teacher, the lesson is that "the only way to get a thing done is to start to do it, then keep on doing it, and finally you'll finish it, even if in the beginning you think you can't do it at all"; from Miss Weimer he learns that "there are ways of saying or doing things, which may not be the currently approved ways, yet that can be very true and beautiful ways, that people will come to recognize as such in due time" (BS, 31).

The Big Sea records permanently at least two incidents that demonstrate its author's sensitivity and humanity. The first takes place in Mexico. Hughes' father, a callous Black capitalist who disdains the poor and the nonwhite, insists that Indians never appreciate anything (BS, 44). In disbelieving him, Hughes gives cigarettes and a bed to Maximiliano, the Indian servant. The Indian, in return, teaches Hughes to ride a horse without a saddle and to tell a badly worn serape from a good one.

The second incident occurs on the freighter when two African women sneak aboard and thereby incite an orgy. After each sexual act, one of them asks for "Mon-nee'! Mon-nee!" Although the men have none, they continue to use her in turn. Because Hughes responds emotionally to this scene, the autobiographical self almost appears clearly, yet the potential moment vanishes unfulfilled. In sympathizing with the victim, he fails to evaluate: "Finally, I couldn't bear to hear her crying 'Mon-nee!' anymore, so I went to bed. But the festival went on all night" (BS, 108). This failure to create a fully autobiographical self recurs when Hughes is silent about his later affair with the Russian dancer Si-lan (Sylvia) Chen."

If he is vague about his sexual life, he is concrete about his reviewers. *The Big Sea* preserves a world in which Hughes understands Black critics better than they understand him. He re-

alizes why they react hostilely to *Fine Clothes to the Jew*. He knows
that Octavus Roy Cohen caricatures Blacks in his stories, that
Thomas Dixon's books abuse Blacks, that contemporary movies
make Blacks into servants or clowns. But this does not change
his purpose of immortalizing an actual folk: "I personally knew
very few people anywhere who were wholly beautiful and wholly
good. . . . I didn't know the upper class Negroes well enough to
write much about them. I knew only the people I had grown up
with, and they weren't people whose shoes were always shined,
who had been to Harvard, or who had heard of Bach. But they
seemed to me good people, too. . . . Curiously enough, a short
ten years later, many of those very poems in *Fine Clothes to the
Jew* were being used in Negro schools and colleges" (BS, 267-
68).

Hughes passes up two other opportunities to create a distinct
autobiographical self. His break with his patron, the major crisis
of the book, is one. The old woman has set him up in a suburban
apartment and has put his brother in school in New England.
She has given him "fine bond paper for writing" (BS, 316) and
a filing case for his papers; she has furnished a typist and fine
clothes as well. Now Hughes has immediate access to theaters,
operas, and lectures. Content at having finished *Not without
Laughter*, he has written nothing since, for he writes only when
feeling unhappy. Hughes cannot forget the images of people
sleeping in subways, and the beggars who appear in every block
disturb him. He begins to rise to the occasion, to reach that
epiphany from which he can understand both his patron and
himself: "She wanted me to be primitive and know and feel the
intuitions of the primitive. But, unfortunately, I did not feel the
rhythms of the primitive surging through me, and so I could not
live and write as though I did. . . . So, in the end it all came
back very near to the old impasse of white and Negro again,
white and Negro—as do most relationships in America." But
Hughes lets the moment pass without the masterful achievement
that might have been: "I cannot write here about the last half-
hour in the big bright drawing-room high above Park Avenue

one morning, because when I think about it, even now, something happens in the pit of my stomach that makes me ill" (*BS*,
325).

In an enduring moment, Hughes chooses to lose many ameni-
ties of the world but to regain his soul. Yet he never articulates
this awareness. In the early winter of 1930 he broke irreparably
with Mrs. Mason. He had loved her kindness and generosity,
including her sincere support for Black advancement and liberal
causes, yet they had disagreed profoundly on political philosophy
and race. Mason believed that the expression of political opinions
should be left to white people like herself, and that Black artists
should be a cultural exoticism in the United States—in other
words, link whites to the primitive life. But Hughes, seeing the
economics of the oppressed Blacks, wrote instead a leftist poem,
"Advertisement for Opening of the Waldorf-Astoria" (*New
Masses*, Jan. 1935), attacking the luxury hotel "where no Negroes
worked and none were admitted as guests."

Following the break with Mrs. Mason, Hughes moved to
Cleveland in December because his mother was living there with
Homer Clark. Earlier, he and Zora Neale Hurston had agreed
that he would construct the plot and develop the characters for
a play to be called *Mule Bone*; she would do the dialogue and
work on an authentic southern tone and nuance. By May 1930,
with Louise Thompson as typist, the collaborators had completed
the first and third acts and a part of the second, and Hurston
took the draft south with her for the summer. She stayed until
November, while Hughes worked on his own play, *Mulatto*, and
was preoccupied by the publication and mixed reception of *Not
without Laughter*, which appeared in July.

In Cleveland, in severe ill health, unable to afford surgery for
the tonsillitis that had kept him in bed over Christmas, and
unable to get a job there in those Depression days, Hughes learned
in January 1931 from his old friends the Jelliffes, directors of
Karamu House, that they and their Gilpin Players, America's
oldest Black theater group, had been offered an excellent Black
comedy—*Mule Bone*, by Zora Hurston. The ensuing conflict,

with its agreements and recantations, reads like a rather grim farce, with Hurston finally saying that she had called the play exclusively hers because Hughes would only spend his half of the royalties on some girl she disliked—meaning Louise Thompson. The play, at one point titled *A Bone of Contention*, was never produced, though part of Act 3 was published in *Drama Critique* in the spring of 1964.

Whatever the break between Hughes and Hurston, he had shared with her a profound interest in the conversion of folk experience into the imaginative celebration of Black American culture. Early in his narrative Hughes writes: "Through my grandmother's stories always life moved, moved heroically toward an end. Nobody ever cried in my grandmother's stories. They worked, or schemed, or fought. But no crying. When my grandmother died, I didn't cry, either. Something about my grandmother's stories (without her ever having said so) taught me the uselessness of crying about anything" (*BS*, 17). To say that Hughes had his grandmother in mind when writing "Aunt Sue's Stories" (*Crisis*, July 1921) would be to conjecture where one cannot prove. It would be more logical to say that this poem, like the autobiographical memoir, shows a child's respect for an elder and the same theme of enlightenment:

> And the dark-faced child, listening,
> Knows that Aunt Sue's stories are real stories.
> He knows that Aunt Sue never got her stories
> Out of any book at all,
> But that they came
> Right out of her own life. [*SP*, 6]

Nor can we say, since we are unable to read the thoughts of dead men, that Hughes' decision to avoid suicide at seventeen resulted in the poem "Life Is Fine" (*One-Way Ticket*, 1949).

> I went down to the river,
> I set down on the bank.
> I tried to think but couldn't

So I jumped in and sank
. . . .
I could've died for love—
But for livin', I was born.   [SP, 121]

But we can say that his decision not to shoot himself in Mexico
(BS, 47) celebrates life indirectly. He remembers that he has yet
to see the ranch, to visit the top of the volcano, and to attend
the bullfights; he has neither graduated from high school nor
married (which he will never do). Since life offers almost infinite
possibilities, he goes on in hope.

The narrator of "Note on Commercial Theater" (Crisis, March
1940) criticizes those who exploit Black art, just as the Hughes
of The Big Sea finds fault with Gladys Bentley: "The old magic
of the woman and the piano and the night and the rhythm being
one is gone. But everything goes, one way or another. The '20s
are gone and lots of things in Harlem night life have disappeared
like snow in the sun—since it became utterly commercial,
planned for the downtown tourist trade, and therefore dull" (BS,
226). And,

> You've taken my blues and gone—
> You sing 'em on Broadway
> And you sing 'em in Hollywood Bowl,
> And you mixed 'em up with symphonies
> And you fixed 'em
> So they don't sound like me.
> Yep, you done taken my blues and gone.   [SP, 190]

The narrator of Hughes' short story "Slave on the Block"
(Scribner's Magazine, Sept. 1933; WF, 19-32) tells a humorous
story about the mischievous servant Luther, an "object of art"
who prompts his own dismissal, mocking subtly the Carraway
belief in primitivism, just as the Hughes of The Big Sea criticizes
his patron's ideas. Oceola Jones, the Black pianist in "The Blues
I'm Playing" (WF, 96-120), breaks with her white patron, too:
Mrs. Ellsworth wants Oceola to play primitive music, and Oceola

wants to play blues and the classics as well. Though Hughes' art does not need his life invariably for appreciation or illumination, for his art often stands almost alone, the values in *The Big Sea* pervade much of his more imaginative literature.

The revisions of *The Big Sea*, which was written in three drafts, demonstrate a conscious effort to enhance the mythic depths of the story. [12] What began as a banal description of Maupassant sharpens in the first revision: "then all of a sudden the beauty and the meaning . . . came to me." Hughes added that he "wandered" by his father, who sought him at the train station and in the streets. What unifies the amendments is the dynamic life that transcends stasis and safety: not the "tons of falling water," as in the original, but the "tons of falling water washed . . . " Even Josephine Baker, the "perfect piece of African sculpture," had to have her animation written in. Where the original draft portrayed the commercial corruption of the achievements in the Harlem Renaissance, the author's revisions mark the brilliance of his own voice. Whatever Baker's magic, time would tarnish it, but a talent had radiated from within her as well as him; in conflict with the permanency of the universe, *"everything"* [my italics] *"goes."* Analogous to the seasons, the 1920s had *passed* (my italics) "like snow in the sun." Where the writer had settled at first for mundane description, he used finally the force in verbs. The vague phrase "Fantastic period in Harlem" transformed itself into the more concrete clause "When Harlem was in vogue," retaining but reinvigorating the passing of time and the evolution of consciousness, particularly what linked historical events in a definable sequence concealing itself as myth.

The myth of Eleonora Duse as the fallen artist had to be written into the second revision. "Then she began to speak. But her voice was lost, and somehow the magic didn't come through. Even when she lifted her famous hands, in the vastness of the Metropolitan Opera House that night the magic didn't come through. She seemed just a tiny little old woman, on an enormous stage, speaking in a foreign language, before an audience that didn't understand. After a while, behind me some of the people began to drift out and it was not so crowded among the standees. Before it was over, there was plenty of room" (BS, 131).

As regards place and alienation in the drafts, "The people were restless. . . . [They] pressed against my back" and "coughed on my shoulders" were highly effective amendments (BS, 131). While in both the first and second revisions, Hughes—down and out in Paris—vows never to ask his father for help even if he, Langston, should die of malnutrition, the second draft finishes with "on the steps of the Louvre" (BS, 151).

And what, indeed leads Hughes to look beneath the cosmetic veneer that Alain Locke, who could read the city "like a book," directs him toward in Venice?

> Dr. Locke knew Venice like a book. He knew who had painted all the pictures, and who had built all the old buildings, and where Wagner had died. He also knew the good restaurants for eating, and was gracious enough to invite me to dine with him.
>
> But before the week was up, I got a little tired of palaces and churches and famous paintings and English tourists. And I began to wonder if there were no back alleys in Venice and no poor people and no slums and nothing that looked like the districts down by the markets on Woodland Avenue in Cleveland, where the American Italians lived. So I went off by myself a couple of times and wandered around in sections not stressed in the guide books. And I found that there were plenty of poor people in Venice and plenty of back alleys off canals too dirty to be picturesque. [BS, 189-90]

Though the professor knows the painters of the pictures and the makers of "all the old buildings," Hughes seeks the artistic self that had given life to the artifacts.

The revisions of Big Sea demonstrate clearly Hughes' attempt to convert the personal history of 1902-31 into the public myths of loneliness, time, and eternal return. His amendments include reflections on his mother, on racial discrimination in Cleveland during 1918, and on the meaning in the stories of Maupassant. They reshape, his thoughts about his parents' divorce and his stay with his father in Mexico during 1919 as well as his sadness about the abuse of the two African girls aboard ship back in 1923. His representation of the sea as dynamic and sublime motion bolsters the description of the third mate, who has made the voyage twenty-nine times. The revision alters the narrator's description to read not "many years" but "always."

Whatever his limits as an autobiographer, Langston Hughes sought to enhance the mythic and personal dimensions of the text. While the deeper reading of the final version requires a reorientation of the seemingly ancient discussions about Black American autobiography as history and narrative, the clear discernment of the tradition supports the reevaluation. During some impressive moments of figuration, the life of Frederick Douglass's seems embodied in the fight with the slave breaker, Covey, in Paganini's violin, or in the weary climb up the old pyramids; each image contributes to symbolic movements of social defiance, art, and time. When some clandestine night riders destroy the press of Ida B. Wells in Memphis, they really want to undermine her adamant resolve. For Richard Wright the autobiographical awareness takes place when a white employer, a woman, says he will never become a writer. In Notes of a Native Son, James Baldwin throws a glass of water at a waitress who reminds him dramatically of Jim Crow in Princeton. Maya Angelou focuses on her rape as a child. Ann Moody discovers a beautiful self in the mirror. So compelled toward lyric awareness, each persona freezes a figurative moment from narrative history.

When Langston Hughes dreams of writing stories about Blacks which one would read even after after his death, he implies that his immortality rests not on a treatment of himself but on a realistic portrayal of others. What W.E.B. Du Bois, one of his mentors during the Renaissance and beyond, might have told him is that the self yearns finally to imprint its own design on history. Where Hughes keeps the images of Alain Locke, Wallace Thurman, Jessie Fauset, and Zora Hurston better than he saves his own, we struggle to break through the maze of muddled chronology to find the created self that strikes occasionally the note of true autobiography. But the Hughes imagined only hints at appearing, falls back into obscure silence, and observes events as they unfold. The narrator of *The Big Sea* neither engages himself fully in social and historical scenes nor interprets their meaning and significance. How does a truly humble and private man create an imagined self that illustrates well his privacy and humility? The public Hughes is vague because the private Hughes is great, precisely at the juncture between self and history.

When Hughes stayed on the top floor of the Alianza de Intelectuales in Madrid in 1937, his room faced the fascist guns directly (*WW*, 333). In the recurring pattern of literary relations, he met more white American writers than ever before. Hemingway and Martha Gelhorn were already in Madrid; playwright Lillian Hellman and critic Malcolm Cowley would join them. Sometimes both Nancy Cunard and the poet-critic Stephen Spender turned up as well. So did non-English-speaking writers such as the French novelist André Malraux, and Pablo Neruda, the leftist poet from Chile. Hughes, who returned to Paris by train, got there in time for Christmas and for talk of war. It was a grim new year.

Russian intellectuals told Hughes that Spain was only a training ground for Hitler and Mussolini, a country for bombing practice by fascist pilots, and impending World War II would be everywhere. When Jacques Roumain (an old friend from the Haiti days) claimed that the world would end, Langston quipped, "I doubt it . . . and if it does, I intend to live to see what happens." "You Americans," Roumain said, shaking his head (*WW*, 401). But Hughes still drew upon the optimism of his dead grandmother even then. "What's the matter with you boy?" she had once asked him. "You can't expect every apple to be a perfect apple. Just because it's got a speck on it, you want to throw it away. Bite that speck out and eat that apple, son. It's still a good apple." The writer reflects: "That's the way the world is . . . bite the specks out . . . still a good apple" (*WW*, 402). The poet, he understood intuitively, was not only the inhabitant of history but the interpreter of it as well: "But that is what I want to be, a writer, recording what I see, commenting upon it, and distilling from my own emotions a personal interpretation" (*WW*, 400-401).

During the Spanish Civil War in 1937, the famous flamenco singer La Niña de los Peines, Pastora Pavón, had a lasting influence on his creative thought. As her bluesy art resisted both war and death, she, like him, was an artist who signified human courage.[13] When Hughes heard that she had refused to leave Madrid, he prepared himself to enter the besieged city. There he saw her at eleven o'clock one morning when she appeared on a bare stage among guitarists who clapped their hands and tapped their heels. Sitting straight in a chair, this old woman began slowly to dominate the performance with her half-spoken and half-sung *solea*. As the guitars played behind her, the poet listened only to that wild, hard, harsh, lonely, and bittersweet voice. Hughes, who would hear La Niña sing many times, compared her flamenco to Black southern blues because, despite the heartbreak implied, it signified the triumph of a people. La Niña, in a sense, was Hughes' gypsy self, for beyond the detachment of Duse, the realism of Maupassant, and the narrative consciousness of Lawrence, her spiritual intensity captivated the Black poet. It reminded him that great art subsumes and transcends great pain.

Yet to retrace Langston Hughes' biography means to go beyond what he and others have written well. From 1918 through 1940 his lyric imagination overcame, or at least ignored, the collapse of a personal American dream; from 1941 through 1961 (*Ask Your Mama*) it struck an ironic balance between the dream and social injustice; as social reality demanded a high price from 1962 through 1967, it waned. Langston Hughes' biography and autobiography translate themselves into the enduring metaphors and thoughts of the writer's creative life. These include the fall of modern man and the American Eden; the physical and spiritual hunger that mark the human epic; the early rejection, even neglect, and ultimate reaffirmation of books and therefore of education; the necessity, quest, and doubt of both personal and human meaning; and the transitory intensity of memory and reflection as the means to sustain an artistic imagination.

Though any one of his suggestive metaphors or ideas merits a study in its own right, I have chosen to focus on Peines and Sano and on the sensitive narrator who recreates as well as preserves them. Through such complexly symbolic figures, Hughes imposed Black American blues, a lyric transcendence over tragic history, upon the record of one war in Spain and another around the globe. The autobiographical self, partly divided between history and a purer art, is sometimes as paradoxical as the mirroring selves it seeks to capture in narrative, or those to which it is so inescapably bound. Hughes's historical images, as emblems of creative imagination, prepare us well to read "Mother to Son," "Madrid—1937," and "Shadow of the Blues." What concerns us is finally no simplistic discussion of types or characters in and of themselves. It is, on the contrary, the creative coherence between them and the poetic voice often beyond as well as with them. It is the pattern of artistic evolution and the personal struggle to extend the very limits of autobiography, a narrative measure of limited time. It is what must bind the lyricist finally to the tragicomedian.

2

THE "CRYSTAL STAIR" WITHIN
The Apocalyptic Imagination

Langston Hughes empowered his various renditions of the Black woman with a double-edged vision. At once it heroically faced the Jim Crow discrimination in the early part of the twentieth century, taking in some comic detachment as well, and showed Blacks transcending the social limitations some whites would impose upon them. What Hughes sensed in the folk source of woman was the dynamic will to epic heroism in both the physical and spiritual dimensions, and while the compulsion revealed itself in varying forms—the disciplined application to labor, the folk trickery that allows comic wit to circumvent defeat, the direct act of social defiance—Black woman incarnated the complex imagination and the masks through which it appeared. When her presence declined in his poetry, as in "Madrid—1937" and "Down Where I Am" (*Voices*, 1950), power and hope diminished somewhat as well. Whether in *The Ways of White Folks* (1934), *The Best of Simple* (1961), or the most telling of the short fiction, the eventual secularization of her previously religious image would increase irony as well as comic distance in the work. Though it was appropriate to Hughes' largesse, as an ethical writer, to restore complex humanity to Black woman in particular and woman in general, he had to replace the great void she had once occupied as idol and type. Then he would have to look at her as the well-rounded human being she was.

Even in the great lyrics such as "The Negro Speaks of Rivers" (*Crisis*, June 1921) and "Daybreak in Alabama" (*Unquote*, June 1940), where woman disappears as a persona, her symbolic yet invisible presence pervades (to speak in Hughes' metaphors) the fertility of the earth, the waters, and the rebirth of the morning. To trace the complex and rich design of woman in his world means to understand the symbolic movements enacted through the passage of his entire career, with varying degrees of free play back and forth from the great lyrics and monologues ("Mother to Son," *Crisis*, 1922), through his melodramas ("Father and Son," 1934; *Mulatto*, 1934-35) and comic detachments (the Madam poems; *One-Way Ticket*, 1949). The poems on women help to establish an overview for all his succeeding genres. They lead from his lighter humor and cryptic "warning" to white America in 1951 finally to the brilliant and underestimated stream of consciousness (*Ask Your Mama*, 1961), subsuming yet transcending them all.

For Langston Hughes the metaphor of woman marks the rise from the historical source, the folk expression of his grandmother in 1910, to the Civil Rights movement and the white backlash in late 1967. For Hughes, Black woman in particular signifies the cycle through which the poetic imagination emerges from history and transcends it but, as in "Fancy Free" (a tale of Simple), falls back to earth or history.[1]

In a statement by Maud Bodkin, one of the ablest critics of Hughes' time, we find a way to read some of his most accomplished poems. Bodkin explains the function of the female image in literature:

> Following the associations of the figure of the muse as communicated in Milton's poetry, we have reached a representation of yet wider significance—the figure of the divine mother appearing in varied forms, as Thetis mourning for Achilles, or Ishtar mourning and seeking for Tammuz. In

this mother and child pattern the figure of the child, or youth, is not distinctively of either sex, though the male youth appears the older form. In historical times, the pattern as it enters poetry may be present, either as beautiful boy or warrior—Adonis, Achilles—or as maiden—Prosperine, Kore—an embodiment of youth's bloom and transient splendor. In either case, the figure appears as the type-object of a distinctive emotion—a complex emotion within which we may recognize something of fear, pity and tender admiration, such as a parent may feel, but "distanced," as by relation to an object universal, an event inevitable.[2]

Not only does the code make for the coherence in "Mother to Son" (1922) and "The Negro Mother" (1931), possibly the two most famous of the matriarchal verses, but the exploration extends to some of the less well-known poems, thereby helping reveal finally the code of faith and redemption in contemporary American literature and thought.

"Mother to Son" begins the strong matriarchal portraits found in Hughes' poetry and fiction.[3] In twenty lines of dramatic monologue a Black persona addresses her son. Making clear the hardships of Black life, she asserts the paradox of the American mythmakers, who propose that all Americans are equal. Subsequently, she acknowledges the personal and racial progress through her metaphor of ascent. In a powerful refrain she teaches the child her moral of endurance as well as triumph: "And life for me ain't been no crystal stair."

Structurally, the poem provides the folk diction and rhythm that make the woman real: "Well, son, I'll tell you: / Life for me ain't been . . . " To simulate the inflections of Black colloquialisms, the individual lines skillfully blend anapestic, iambic, and trochaic cadences:

> But all the time
> I'se been a-climbin' on
> And reachin' landin's

And turnin' corners
And sometimes goin' in the dark
Where there ain't been no light.

Varied in syllabic length, the lines have ten, nine, eight, and seven cadences; others have four, three, and one.

So boy, don't you turn back
Don't you set down on the steps
'Cause you finds it's kinder hard.

[Note: Cadences per my ear]

Don't you fall now—
For I'se still goin', honey,
I'se still climbin',
And life for me ain't been no crystal stair.

Although the last line is iambic, the meter of the poem depends more on the noted simulation of Black rhetoric, the actual cadences of folk speech, than on metric form.[4]

In "Mother to Son" the complex of Christian myth informs the portrait of the woman. As a figure of mythic ascent, she becomes only typologically at one with the Vergil of the *Divine Comedy* or the Christ of the New Testament. But she is neither a great and ancient poet nor a god incarnate; rather, she is Woman struggling to merge with godhead. In more than making her way from failure to success, she moves from a worldly vision to a religious one, for hers is less a progression of the body than an evolution of the soul. Her last line—"And life for me ain't been no crystal stair"—repeats and reinforces her second. Yet through the power of her will and imagination, she has endowed the world far more richly by her inner light than society ever bequeathed opportunities to her. While the social world hardly ennobles her, she nevertheless ennobles it, and the quality of her grandeur marks the depth of her humanity. She cautions her son, "Don't you fall now." Because she associates the quest with her divine vision, any separation from it implies the fallen world, demarcating in itself the descent from heavenly grace.

While Christian myth is central to its complexity of meanings, the poem implies the interwoven designs of quest and self-realization. With the past participle of the durative verb *be*, the mother tells her offspring, "I's been a-climbin' on."[5] As the vertical ascent anticipates her continued ascent, it looks forward to temporary success or to a respite from future quest ("reachin' landin's and turnin' corners").

Shrouded in religious myth, the Black woman must still confront secular reality, and the tension reveals the idea of Black oppression. The building, that synecdochical and metaphysical sign, becomes life itself as well as the questionable belief in any cosmic order. Dilapidated boards and bare feet imply the presence of deprivation or poverty in the house. Because the mother lived literally in a building that had loose tacks and splinters, she risked physical penetration and infection throughout her life. Yet she has withstood any fatal injury to the Black American soul. Her internal light illuminates the outer world.

"The Negro Mother" (*SP*, 288-89) resembles "Mother to Son" in code but differs from it in form. Once more the mixture of iambic and anapestic feet appears, while the rhythm results in a simulation of Black rhetoric.

> Children, I come back today
> To tell you a story of the long dark way
> That I had to climb, that I had to know
> In order that the race might live and grow
> Look at my face—dark as the night—
> Yet shining like the sun with love's true light.

Here the tetrameter and pentameter lines give a formal consistency.

"The Negro Mother" facilitates the division of itself into three parts. The first introduces the reader to the spirit or ghost of the mother, who represents the racial as well as historical consciousness of Blacks. In addressing her children or symbolic posterity, the mother identifies herself. The second shows that the mother's religious faith enabled her to endure adversity. Here she stands apart from her own monologue, and the moment becomes her awed reminiscence of personal accomplishment more than a speech to any particular listener.

I couldn't read then. I couldn't write.
I had nothing, back there in the night.
Sometimes, the valley was filled with tears,
But I kept trudging on through the lonely years.

In spirit the mother merges with her children to guarantee continued racial success. Part two prepares skillfully for part three, through which she returns from introspection to express herself in direct address once again. In the last section she cautions Blacks about the barriers still ahead: "Remember how the strong in struggle and strife / Still bar you the way . . ."

Myth means, in this instance, the religious overtones that cloak the parent-to-child monologue, implying pilgrimage. In opposing secular history—namely, the woman's being stolen from Africa—the tone heightens the tension between the real and the ideal. When the mother remembers the selling of her children after she "crossed the wide sea," the biblical cadence may remind the auditor of the human wanderings in Exodus.

The second part shows a shift in emphasis from the mother to the children who must continue the sacred quest. To express her belief in right, she prepares them by using metaphor, simile, and echo: "But God put a song and a prayer in my mouth. / God put a dream like steel in my soul." In identifying with a Christian woman, Hughes demonstrates his talent to create an autonomous persona. While more personal poems such as "Who but the Lord" indicate his own Christian humanism, as opposed to the mother's even deeper religiosity, her faith in the second part prepares for the lines near the end of the third: "Oh, my dark children, may my dream and my prayers / Impel you forever up the great stairs."

Christian images help to reveal her code of heroic sacrifice.

When Hughes concentrates Christian images in the second and final sections, the "valley" complements the journey's "road." Subsequently, the narration lays out the goals and blessings that the mother urges the children to take. When she tells them to "look ever upward," the closure suggests once more the spatial duality that suggests both an embarkment and a place of departure. As in "Mother to Son," linear and vertical distances merge in the Christian metaphor of travel. Where she encourages the children to climb the "great stairs," she enhances the implication of ascent. Like the dilapidated stair in "Mother to Son," these stairs imply racial quest as well.

The female figure in "Negro Mother" functions much like that in "Mother to Son," for in being mythic it becomes a foil to secular reality. From an opposition of divine quest and earthly limitation emerges the theme of social restriction. The reader imagines the longevity of Black suffering in the United States for three hundred years. During that time, experience forged the "dream like steel" in the mother's soul; consequently, the dream inspired her to survive a valley "filled with tears" and a road "hot with sun." Though she has been beaten and mistreated, and though she warns her offspring that racial restrictions still exist, her spirit has triumphed. While we do not know the strength of the bars that represent the limitations in the third part, the tone suggests that these surpass neither the will of the mother nor the potential strength of the children whom she inspires. That in the second part the mother overcame her inability to read and write supports this reading. So do the sweat, pain, and despair she remembers in the third part, after having transcended them. She has withstood the whip of the slaver's lash. In combining social limits with Christian myth, Hughes uses his alliterative skill in fusing liquids with plosives: "Remember how the strong in struggle and strife / still bar you the way . . ."

In helping to illuminate the design of social confinement, the Black woman serves a third and equally important function; indeed, the imagery and idea of Nature rely on her presence. Pictures of light and dark, plants that grow or seeds that imply growth, all signify that presence—as does any place of growth. To unify the different parts as sections within an organic whole, Hughes distributes five images of the kind in the first part and three in the second as well as in the third. For example, the mother speaks of the "long dark way" that anticipates her self-reminiscence as the "dark girl." In the latter instance she becomes the image of the Black race transported across the sea. The darkness of the traveled way and the female figure who must travel it through time fuse with diurnal cycle. Consequently, the Black woman expresses the past in cyclic metaphor: "I had nothing, back there in the night," yet her advice to others will make for a different future, one of heroic progress as her "banner" is lifted from the "dust"—another echo of Christian myth, alluding to Ecclesiastes and suggesting mortality. In the third part the mother instructs her children to make of her past a "torch for tomorrow," thus teaching them the secret of Black art: the conversion of suffering into personal and social good. In lighting her way, the torch signals moral progression.

A natural complex unifies the first and second parts in "The Negro Mother." Like corn and cotton the Black race grows, though the analogy is ambiguous. While the products described grow for the purpose of human consumption, Hughes implies that the Black race develops in order to end exploitation. As corn and cotton grew in the field in which the mother worked, suffering enhanced her wisdom as well as her spirit. In tending the field outside herself, she nourished within herself the dream and seed of the free.

Other natural icons show that the unity of the poem depends upon the maternal portrait. The mother's general delineation as woman early on prepares for the particular depiction of her as the "Negro mother" in the second and third parts. Because, in the second part, the woman is the seed of an emerging free race, she becomes one with her children, who are young and free. Similarly, the Black woman's advice in the third part displays both her courage and the bond between a woman and her descendants: "Stand like free men." The banner that she urges her offspring to lift shares the firmness of her imperative verb, "stand." The first part makes clear the mother's place in the lineage of Black people, as through internal rhyme the color of her face blends with the history of the race.

Other poems about women preceded or followed "The Negro Mother"; "Mother to Son" is probably the most famous of the earlier verses and the "Madam Poems" the most memorable of the subsequent ones. The image of woman operates throughout these works in at least eleven diverse ways, which are not always separable. 1) In signaling stories about her yesterdays, 2) woman survives adversity and triumphs spiritually as well as artistically. 3) She presents an opportunity to admire the splendor of youth now departed or 4) to characterize a folk life-style of vibrant flare and color. 5) In providing a portrait of trouble, she cannot transcend adversity sometimes, but 6) she converts suffering into transcendence. 7) Sometimes she signifies the heavy yet affirmative tone through which humanity sublimates suffering into art; 8) at other times she clarifies a secular persona's comic and serious confrontation with death. 9) Even in emphasizing the dramatic situation of a deserted wife and 10) a matriarchal society, she 11) incarnates heroic determination.

The poems themselves illustrate the different functions quite well. The title characters in "Aunt Sue's Stories" (*Crisis*, July 1921, 121; *SP*, 6) and "Mexican Market Woman" are natural foils to each other. Having survived adversity, Aunt Sue tells a Black boy stories about the past (see Chapter 1), and though she tells them as fiction, he knows that they are true as well. While only his imagination seems at first to confirm the authenticity of her mythmaking, history does indeed verify her story as the narrative self renders it clearly. If the listening boy has not yet lived a generation through Black American history, the speaking self almost surely has even by 1921. Not entirely parallel with the narrated world, his own now silent history marks an oblique angle toward her very credible fiction and toward historical truth. He mediates, in other words, between her imaginative world and the world of history, the latter deferred only by the lyrical power

of the poem itself. Unlike Aunt Sue, the Mexican market woman
remembers the joy of her past.

> This ancient hag
> Who sits upon the ground
> Selling her scanty wares
> Day in, day round,
> Has known high wind-swept mountains,
> and the sun has made
> Her skin so brown.

Though the female figure in "Troubled Woman" (SP, 77), a
short lyric of sorrow based on brilliant similes, is less transcendent
than is Aunt Sue, the narrator achieves rhythmic success. Almost
as a religious chant, here is a subdued form of the Black folk
sermon.

> Bowed by
> Weariness and pain
> Like an
> Autumn flower
> In the frozen rain,
> Like a
> Windblown autumn flower
> That never lifts its head
> Again.

At first the persona in "Strange Hurt" (SP, 84) probably seems
masochistic. Some man has deserted a woman, and

> In months of snowy winter
> When cozy houses hold,
> She'd break down doors
> To wander naked
> In the cold.

The woman, losing love or a part of spiritual reality, becomes
indifferent to physical reality. Remarkably, the poem displays the

ability to subsume and transcend fear through confrontation. Stormy weather, burning sunlight, and snowy winter mark the physical harm that Black Americans face. To stand without fear against the elements is to be free in spirit.

In one reading, "Cora" (*SP*, 146) renders the racial dilemma nearly allegorically:

> I broke my heart this mornin',
> Ain't got no heart no more.
> Next time a man comes near me
> Gonna shut an' lock my door
> Cause they treat me mean—
> The ones I love.
> They always treat me mean.

Is a chance for true love (any more than the liberal belief in human fellowship) worth the risk of renewed despair? While Cora tells the story of her love life realistically, she incarnates the ambivalence of the race. Because a man broke Cora's heart this morning, she refuses rhetorically ever to try love again, yet her tone suggests a tantrum more than a certitude. While Hughes' analogy is subtle, it is sure as well. Insofar as the race pouts, it tires of the irreparable hurt imposed by history (even as the literary imagination imposes itself conversely upon this very same history), from the burden of seeking humanity constantly. But perhaps Blacks will try again? Are the words "Gonna shut an' lock my door" ironic or straight?[6]

Over time, Hughes diversified the design of the Divine Mother into some broader treatments that are heroic, comic, and despairing. As the years wore on, he had to free the image from religious myth. In part, the change depends on his own diminishing optimism. When "Southern Mammy Sings" (*Poetry*, 1941) bridges "Mother to Son" (1922) and "Down Where I Am" (1950), the speaker has lapsed from energetic hope into overpowering fatigue a generation later. Tone and sense reverse themselves drastically:

Too many years
Climbin' that hill,
'Bout out of breath.
I got my fill.

I'm gonna plant my feet
On solid ground.
If you want to see me,
Come down.[7]

Hughes, with a whimper far more than a bang, brings to a close his lifelong preoccupation with the transcendent myth of woman only indirectly. "Southern Mammy" marks the turning point because he uses the female figure there to represent spiritual as well as physical exhaustion: she despairs because whites have hanged a "colored boy" whose only crime was saying people should be free. The "southern mammy" herself is an allegorical foil to the "Miss Gardner," "Miss Yardman," and "Miss Michaelmas" she mentions, though each of those women personifies a place in a way that "mammy" does not do at all. Having no place in the country or world, the alienated servant has seen the death of her sons; now she anticipates only war and death, "And I am gettin' tired!" (SP, 162).

Often The "Madam" poems[8] embody folk themes in dialogue, though at least one of them, "Madam and the Phone Bill" (SP, 208), uses dramatic monologue. As a whole, the group humorously illuminates the ideas of nationalism, self-reliance, and self-doubt, while the secular world supplants the mythic one for good. "Madam and the Fortune Teller" (SP, 211), for example, is a particularly skillful poem of the kind. Here the teller would impart self-determination to the auditor and customer, but the customer, unwilling to accept the humanistic burden, continues to press for divine intervention. When the teller refuses to give her any, the listener shifts the ground impatiently to another external "power": "What man you're talking 'bout?" Now aware that the auditor declines to apprehend the truth, the teller asks for another dollar and a half before she proceeds to read the other palm. As the folk ballad goes, the teller sure "picked poor robin clean"—but only because Robin refuses to live without illusion. What Langston Hughes dramatized so brilliantly in the auditor he must have discerned finally about himself and humanity. In the pursuit of some external decision, the seeker overlooks her own responsibility on earth. She needs always the sign of something beyond, the absent ideal of which the present realism reminds us only indirectly. Whereas the early poems mark, sometimes dramatically, an ascent from earth to heaven, the later ones embody often not only the redescent to earth but the closure of the great stairway. The vertical route that had never existed for woman or anybody else in physical space in the first place withdraws itself back from the external world now to the mind of the poet. In the process he recasts his fictional self as Madam. Though the auditor can read in her cards the obvious fortune only of what the teller narrates forthrightly, the teller reads the deeper irony of the human self ever in struggle with destiny and history. What separates the two women is Madam's human imagination.

In "Mother to Son" and "The Negro Mother," however, which combine Christian myth and folk experience, Langston Hughes becomes one of several American poets to deal with a problem of religious belief. Our literary artists have believed (or disbelieved) in God, the American Dream, the Power of Transcendence, or the American Myth. Edward Taylor and William Cullen Bryant believed in God. Emerson believed in transcendence, and his contemporary, Whitman, believed in himself. Whitman had faith as well in a power that could rejuvenate or at least reinvigorate the world through enthusiastic perception.[9] Wallace Stevens, who was humanistic like Whitman, believed more in man than in external divinity. To Stevens, indeed, man *was* divinity, since divinity must "live within herself."[10] Closer still to our own time, T.S. Eliot, through his Christian conservatism, restored to American poetry a sense of the divine.[11] Alan Ginsberg has laughed at American myth, now putting his "queer shoulder" to the country's wheel.[12]

But no American poet, I think, combines myth and pragmatism better than Langston Hughes does in the poems on women. Indeed, Hughes himself would never do so again. In the 1950s he would turn his attention more to prose than to poetry, and by the 1960s he would lose the sustained intensity of his once lyrical gift, for social injustice would almost never leave either him or his hopeful vision alone. But he never completely abandoned the folk source of his grandmother's stories. They had been the form through which his poetic spirit had taken shape most powerfully. Not always without stereotype, the poems about women were a very special genre for him. Even the most rabid feminist critics could admit that they radiate (whatever the almost inevitable limitations of Man) a profound sympathy and nearly unquestionable love.

Hughes indeed leaves to posterity his myth of the Black female who can tell tales about her yesterdays. Sometimes she becomes a means of discoursing on the youth that is gone forever. At other times, unable to transcend adversity, she personifies trouble sublimated often into art. We must laugh then at her confrontation with death, at her attempts to transcend hardship, if only to avoid crying at her weariness, at the bitterness surrounding the racial quest. But we must admire her heroic imagination. What empowers her creative energy as well as her moral force is the crystal stairway within. She isn't always well-rounded or even professional, but she is still Madam as much as Madonna. She is more human than almost any other female figure inscribed by a Black male writer in either Hughes' time or our own. And with her as a bulwark, we can go on to reconsider his lyrical power more profoundly.

3

"DEEP LIKE THE RIVERS"
The Lyrical Imagination

For many who have rightfully honored Langston Hughes as a cultural historian and poet of the people, the insight of W.R. Johnson, who spoke about the lyrical imagination, could provoke much reconsideration; it would seem indeed inappropriate:

> We want the pictures, yes, but we also want the hates and loves, the blames and the praise, the sense of a living voice, of a mind and heart that are profoundly engaged by a life they live richly, eagerly. Art, then, any art, is not a reproduction of what is seen: it is a highly complex action (action both by artist and audience) in which what is outer and what is inner—things, perceptions, conceptions, actualities, emotions, and ideas—are gathered into and made manifest by emotional and intelligible forms. The artist cannot be undisciplined in searching for such forms . . . he can no more be slovenly in his habits of feeling and thinking than he can be slovenly in his habits of looking and listening or of using the implements of his craft; but neither can he be dispassionate, emotionless, unconcerned. The lie in modern imagism is that no one snaps the picture. But the difference between a bad or mediocre photo and a good or great one is precisely who takes the photo—and the pho-

tographer, like any other artist, is defined not merely by his technique or his mastery of his instrument but also by the quality of his feeling, by the precision and vitality . . . which his composition captures and reveals . . . the thing that called his mind and heart into action.[1]

Still, the words characterize many poems by Langston Hughes, one of Black America's greatest lyricists. Over nearly the last sixty years, during the need to reconsider his contribution to the genre, one has hardly dared think of Hughes in this way for both historical and social reasons. While the Greeks believed the lyric to be a communal performance in song, the shared epiphany between the singer and the audience, the form implied the aristocratic elitism at court during the Middle Ages and the Elizabethan period. In the romantic and Victorian eras, the genre suggested privacy and isolation from the masses. Today, with the genre somewhat diminished in favor of the dramatic monologue, as poetry has possibly ebbed into pedantry, those who prefer personal lyric often disclaim the social rhetoric of direct address. Indeed, one might almost take Langston Hughes at his word and accept the distinction between the forms. But while the margins between genres are convenient, they are yet flexible and partly illusory. Literary forms really mean only variations in degree.

Ironically, Black American history complicates the appreciation of Hughes as a lyricist. In a personal voice the poet revises the tradition he inherited. Where Phillis Wheatley praised George Washington, he honors the Black Everyman and, indeed, Everyperson. Though his contemporary Countee Cullen depended on sources in the poetry of John Keats, Hughes relied on allusions to the folk ballads of 1830-50, on the nature and prophetic poems of Walt Whitman, and on the more contemplative verse of Vachel Lindsay. Paul Laurence Dunbar had accommodated himself earlier to the Old South, but Hughes revised the pastoral for his times (though he was less naive about the folk integrity).

From *Weary Blues* in 1926 to his reprise of "Daybreak in Alabama" at the end of *The Panther and the Lash* in 1967, the lyric serves to open and close Hughes' literary life and work.[2] Though other genres attract his attention, this one retains particular resilience. For him the lyric illuminates the graphic and timeless: "When I get to be a composer / I'm gonna write me some music about / Daybreak in Alabama" (*SP*, 157; *PL*; 101).

Against the backdrop of time, he invokes dynamic feeling in order to subordinate and control personal loneliness, but he never excludes the communal response to social history. In introspection, he plays down the narrative of miscegenation ("Cross," *Crisis*, 1925) and the allegorical tragedy ("Pierrot," *Weary Blues*, 1926) into precise understatement: "So I wept until the dawn / Dripped blood over the eastern hills" (*SP*, 66). Or, sometimes, he disguises the lyrics themselves as dramatic performances through the blues song and the jazz instrument:

> What can purge my heart
>   Of the song
>   And the sadness?
> What can purge my heart
>   Of the sadness
>   Of the song?
>   ["Song for Billie Holiday," *SP*, 102]

What one finds ultimately in the lyricist concerns the sensitive self who speaks to nature and the masses. In an epiphany the solo and the chorus face each other at the height of the performance, itself timeless through intensity and will. Eventually, we redescend from "The Negro Speaks of Rivers" (*Crisis*, 1921) or from "Oppression" (*Fields of Wonder*, 1947) to the fallen world.[3] From the poetic re-creation of Black American history in particular and the American South in general, the narrator returns inevitably to certain death in Harlem, for sequential history is a fact.

For Langston Hughes the lyric highlights the human and social dream. Incarnated in the blues singer and player, it signifies the artistic performance in general:

Beat the drums of tragedy for me,
And let the white violins whir thin and slow,
But blow one blaring trumpet note of sun
To go with me
            to the darkness
                    where I go.[5]
["Fantasy in Purple," *SP*, 103]

Lyric suggests the griot and the cultural priest, who recount the sacred story about experience and the past. From the history of 1855-65, the lyric records the poetic remembrance of the Civil War and of one poet, for instance, who wrote it down.[3]

Old Walt Whitman
Went finding and seeking,
Finding less than sought
Seeking more than found,
Every detail minding
Of the seeking or the finding.   [*SP*, 100]

The speaker, almost indifferent to the historical context, neither mentions whom Whitman met or when, nor says why so. The narrator, excluding the death of Abraham Lincoln, overlooks the troubled circumstances. Still, what he manages involves a frozen moment in self- and human communion.

But the fundamental inquiry into the reconsideration of Hughes as a lyricist depends on a deeper perception of the function of the genre within the structure of his career, especially from 1926 through 1947. Sometimes disguised as the blues performance, his lyric first subsumes social rhetoric into epiphany (*The Weary Blues*, 1926); then encourages inquiry into the technical means for the evocation of awe and wonder, for astonishment, and for the sublime;[4] and finally demonstrates compression and acrostic power (*Fields of Wonder*, (1947). It is convenient to take up the genre according to the dominant themes that unify each of these two volumes.

Largely to assess the significance of the evolution in Hughes' use of the form over at least two decades, it would help us to define further the theory and function of lyric.[5] The genre in-volves poetic emotion which, expressed in time, insists that time itself—or sequential thought—is illusion. Just as the lyric quality displaces the narrative element, so it often represses from itself both intellectual analysis and dramatic action. Yet lyric situates itself well in the dramatic context from which emotion emerges. Though drama takes place in history and time, the lyric distances itself from them. While the drama tends to move dynamically, revealing character and plot as it goes, the lyric stands still. The drama reveals the development of causal action; the lyric illu-minates the progression of emotion. The drama sets into play narrative and historical actions; the lyric expresses the story of the self. At times Langston Hughes succeeds through the pro-jection of the lyric personality into a narrator who speaks and feels truly. The implicit dramatic action depends upon time and space, the particular situation, but the lyric quality suspends them. And though a play such as *Mulatto* (1935) benefits from a precise setting, a poem such as "The Negro Speaks of Rivers" reveals the permanency of memory and human existence:

> I bathed in the Euphrates when dawns were young.
> I built my hut near the Congo and it lulled me to sleep.
> I looked upon the Nile and raised the pyramids above it.
> I heard the singing of the Mississippi when Abe Lincoln
>   went down to New Orleans, and I've seen its muddy
>   bosom turn all golden in the sunset. [*SP*, 4]

However academic the overtones (a detailed explication of "Rivers" for its own sake is more chronologically suited to the discussion below), any elitist assessment of Langston Hughes' lyrics must fail. Open to the range of human emotion, they express misanthropy, egoism, or cynicism.[6] In the display of the solo self, they reveal a concern for the choral one as well.[7] Here the individual talent speaks within cultural and racial tradition. So even Hughes' lyrics are covertly rhetorical. Where poetic

images exist as part of human language, they contribute necessarily to emotive and moral discourse. For the Black American
and social poet, they reconfirm intensely the tension between
the pictured world (American Dream) and the real one (racial
lynching): "A totally unrhetorical poetry will be, as we have
come to know all too well, a poetry void of passion, void of
choosing, void of rational freedom—it will be in Paul Valéry's
metaphor, the rind of the orange without the pulp and the
juice."[8] Even lyric distills the sublime, the humane and social
spirit that informs figurative language: "In our technological so-
cieties, when the individual human began more and more to feel
cut off from his fellows and from the world, when inwardness
became less a matter of anger and terror, the modern choralists,
in their different ways, attempted to countervail this process of
alienation by reaffirming our kinship with each other and with
the world that begets us and nourishes us, by denying that the
exploitations of empire and the degradations worked by the ma-
chine had or would or could succeed."[9]

To recognize the covert rhetoric in lyric means to appreciate
the overlap between emotive and discursive poetry.[10] Rooted in
song, the lyric reestablishes the ritual of human communion.
From the ancients who sang out the odyssey to Woody Guthrie
and Bob Dylan, Roberta Flack and Lionel Richey, the flow con-
tains an inspirational power nearly akin to religion. What one
remembers, finally, concerns the double presence that allows
Langston Hughes to speak at once inside and outside history, to
participate in the dynamic plot yet reflect inertly upon the story,
to read as well as feel the meaning.

For Hughes the lyric imagination bridges the unfallen and
fallen worlds. Aware of the discrepancy between American word
and deed, he hardly mistakes the country itself for the ideal. The
imagination and the social mind separate only in the failure to
impose a coherent vision upon the entire range of human experience. Whereas the tragic *Mulatto* (1935) and the comic *Simple Takes a Wife* (1953) represent the diverse sides present, the
lyrics express the dualism of the whole imagination.

Wave of sorrow
Do not drown me now:
I see the island
Still ahead somehow.   ["Island," SP, 78]

The poems convert fact into value, power into thought, and the
"dualism of word and deed into an orphic unity."[11] While
Hughes' speakers perform historical rites from the Harlem Renaissance, from the Great Depression, from World War II, and
from the Civil Rights movement, they supersede historical sequence. They contain ideals that transcend time (historicity)
and, indeed, Time (human pattern).

> "Words" and "silence" denote two different states of feeling,
> the second higher and purer than the first. Words issue
> from time (tempus) and are vitiated by the penury of our
> daily concerns. However, they know enough to aspire to a
> higher and purer state, given in Eliot's lines as "form" and
> "pattern" in which the mere contents of form are not tran-
> scended but enhanced, fulfilled, redeemed. Silence is there-
> fore a scruple which attends upon the local satisfaction of
> words, the voice which says that words are often self-
> delusions, trivial gratifications. Silence speaks against time
> to redeem time. Silence therefore corresponds to the fine
> excess of the imagination.[12]

Hughes' lyric voice clarifies his own signature to Black American history. Shaped through words, themselves become
symbols,[13] it mediates between antonyms, not completely trans-
latable, into each other, including Black and white, Harlem and
Africa, war and peace:

Help me to shatter this darkness,
To smash this night,
To break this shadow
Into a thousand lights of sun,

Into a thousand whirling dreams
Of sun!   ["As I Grew Older," WB, 55; SP, 11-12]

However apparently private, the lyrics of Langston Hughes im-
plode ultimately into the folk center implied beneath them.
Where the images suggest cultural beliefs and myths, the values
are Black American: "Expressions cannot save us from tempo-
rality, but thanks to symbols, we can ascend to the realm of
eternity."[14] Though Hughes's lyricism displaces the drama and
narrative of Black American history, it signifies nevertheless the
passage from the Harlem Renaissance to the Civil Rights movement. The lyrics imply the very drama that they displace, the
advance from tragedy to peace.[15] Though in these poems Hughes
confines racial suffering and conflict to the half-light, he clarifies the need for reconciliation. What the lyric leaves silent, it
counterplays to for the very power. Langston Hughes, in tracing the lyrical patterns chronologically across his representative volumes of the kind, reclaims from American history
the right to reimagine Black humanity and, indeed, humankind.[16]

A broad overview of The Weary Blues clarifies the thematic
unity and diverse techniques. Grouped according to seven romantic ideas, sixty-eight poems appear under seven headings.
While the emphasis goes to the collective consciousness derived
from African ancestry in particular and human history in general,
other concerns are personal loneliness, isolation, and loss. Still
signifying the Harlem Renaissance and the jazz age, a third set
presents the cabarets, infusing interracial sex within overtones
of the exotic. Indeed, the performance in the title poem (WB,
23-24; SP, 33-34) completes the ritualistic conversion from Black
American suffering into epic communion. On 1 May 1925, during a banquet at an "elegant" Fifth Avenue restaurant in New
York City, the poem won a prize from Opportunity magazine,
where it subsequently appeared. The thirty-five-line lyric presents
a singer and pianist who plays on Harlem's Lenox Avenue one
night. Having performed well in the club, he goes to bed, as the

song still sounds in the mind: "I got de weary blues / And I can't be satisfied." In the "dull pallor of an old gas light," his ebony hands have played on the ivory keys. During the "lazy sway" from the piano stool, he has patted the floor with his feet, struck a few chords, and then sung some more. Finally, he sleeps "like a rock or a man that's dead," the artistic spirit exhausted.[17]

His performance clearly implies several dramatic actions. While one sets the dynamic playing—the Black self-affirmation against what fades—a second presents a vital remaking of the Black self-image. A third shows the transcendence through racial stereotype into lyrical style. From the dramatic situation of the player, both musical as well as performed, the poem imposes isolation and loneliness yet the refusal to accept them. The song marks a metonym for the human imagination. In a deftness often overlooked, Hughes uses anaphora to narrate an imperial self so as to sustain the blues stanza as countermelody and ironic understatement: "Ain't got nobody in all this world, / Ain't got nobody but ma self." What most complements the lyric skill is the dramatic movement of feeling. In narrative distancing his speakers achieve a double identification.

When Hughes' speakers step back from the dramatic performance into the lyric perception, they delimit the space of dream, sometimes in covertly sexual metaphor. At the detached distance from any dramatic situation, they even remake the iconography of Black and white, often revising and neutralizing the traditional code of culture and value.

> To whirl and to dance
> Till the white day is done.
> Then rest at cool evening
> Beneath a tall tree
> . . . .
> A tall, slim tree . . .
> Night coming tenderly
> Black like me. [WB, 42; SP, 14]

Written in two stanzas, "Dream Variations" (first published in *Current Opinion*, September 1924),[18] quoted above, has nine lines in the first and eight in the second, signifying the possible dwindling of the dream. While the persona longs for his dream, he sees the externalization of it in his love for nature, the place, and the sun. What confronts him involves the very dualism of dream, which exists only in the lyric moment of timelessness. While the lyric dream may therefore seem static, it has a meaning finally in the dynamic world of social change, where it would decay. Here the Black self impregnates the lighted world and even Time itself. While the penetrative drive into the Harlem Renaissance, the advance in chronological time, is finite, the receptive response to sentiment or imaginative reassertion remains infinite. Where the Western world asserts the priority of linear time over the natural frontier, the view vanishes ultimately into darkness. Survival depends upon universal harmony with the world: "Night coming tenderly / Black like me." Here the speaker balances the double compulsion toward reason and light ("white day") with the mythic sentiment (dream) that justifies life.

The double identification with penetrative time and receptive timelessness appears perhaps most notably in "The Negro Speaks of Rivers" (*Crisis*, June 1921), a poem dedicated to the late W.E.B. Du Bois. "Rivers" presents the narrator's skill in retracing known civilization back to the source in East Africa. Within thirteen lines and five stanzas, through the suggestion of wisdom by anagoge, we re-project ourselves into aboriginal consciousness. Then the speaker affirms the spirit distilled from human history, ranging from 3000 B.C. through the mid-nineteenth century to the author himself at the brink of the Harlem Renaissance.[19] The powerful repetend "I've known rivers. / Ancient, dusky rivers" closes the human narrative in nearly a circle, for the verse has turned itself subtly from an external focus to a unified and internal one: "My soul has grown deep like the rivers." Except for the physical and spiritual dimensions, the subjective "I" and the "river" read the same.

When the Euphrates flows from eastern Turkey southeast and southwest into the Tigris, it recalls the rise as well as the fall of the Roman Empire. For over two thousand years the water helped delimit that domain. Less so did the Congo, which south of the Sahara demarcates the natural boundaries between white and Black Africa. The latter empties into the Atlantic ocean; the Nile flows northward from Uganda into the Mediterranean; in the United States the Mississippi River flows southeast from north central Minnesota to the Gulf of Mexico. Whether north or south, east or west, "River" signifies the fertility as well as the dissemination of life in concentric half-circles. The liquid, as the externalized form of the contemplative imagination, has both depth and flow. "The Negro Speaks of Rivers" reclaims the origins in Africa of both physical and spritual humanity.

Just as the speaker in "Rivers" stands outside historical time, so the narrator in "Jester" (*Opportunity*, Dec. 1925; WB, 53) distances himself from literary forms as well:

> In one hand
> I hold tragedy
> And in the other
> Comedy—
> Masks for the Soul.

Detached from the dramatic situation, the narrator makes a choral appeal without didacticism, not excluding the epigrammatic twist, abruptly closing the lyric in understatement and rhetorical question. Here appears the invocation to chorus through recovery of the solo:

> Laugh at my sorrow's reign.
> I *am* the Black jester
> The dumb clown of the world,
>
> . . . .
> Once I was wise
> Shall I be wise again?

What some would mistake for simplistic discourse is thoughtful reflection. However much this poem is most telling about the expression of the tragicomic imagination to emerge later in Hughes' world, the piece appears nevertheless in the lyrical form.

While social restrictions ("the wall") existed in 1925, the year "Jester" was first published, they still imply ironically the dream that transcends historical time. The social eclipse appears as "dimming" and "hiding." When dynamism leads finally to stasis, the solo self invokes Nature ("As I Grew Older," WB, 55; SP, 11-12). Where color was descriptive ("my dark hands"), it becomes metaphorical, for any real "darkness" exists within.

Whatever the imminent dangers, the sea provides a means for lyric escape. Written in two stanzas, "Water-Front Streets" (WB, 1; SP, 51) is simply a romantic ballad that shows a movement from external nature to the poetic mind. Hughes achieves a personal revision of the English pastoral tradition. Evolved from Edmund Spenser, the genre was already decadent by the time of Alfred Lord Tennyson, but it subsisted in the lyrics of the Georgians near the turn of the century, just as it does today in confessional and neoromantic poetry. Biographical and autobiographical sources generally note Vachel Lindsay and Amy Lowell as the major traditional influences on Hughes' verse, but the diction and tone here suggest Tennyson's "Crossing the Bar" (1889). The placement of life and death reverses itself: "But lads put out to sea / Who carry their beauties in their hearts / And dreams, like me."

From Milton's "Il Penseroso" to Gray's "Elegy Written in a Country Churchyard," gothic ascent and romantic isolation suggest the evolution of English lyricism. When the sailor (the poet) lifts anchor in "A Farewell" (WB, 72), those on shore hardly miss him because realists lack patience with dreamers. The gypsies and the sailors are metonyms, or the "wanderers of the hills and seas." In seeking the fortune, they leave "folk and fair." For Hughes' speakers, the invoked chorus provides only silence for the "you" who "live between the hills / And have never seen the seas." They counterplay to the poet, Odysseus. In "Seascape" (*WB*, 78; *SP*, 53) Hughes's narrator redescends from lyric heights to sequential history. From a ship off the coast of Ireland, the seamen view a line of fishing ships etched against the sky. Later, off the coast of England, the seamen riding the foam observe "an Indian merchant man coming home." Still, realism infringes upon the dream world. While the seascape is a revelation, the speaker rides in time as well, not merely toward his literal "home" but toward death.[20] For Langston Hughes the lyric arrests the movement of the personal narrative toward extinction. "Death of an Old Seaman" (*WB*, 81) portrays a persona who has returned home. Here he appears against the background of the hill and sea. In facing the winds, he sets into relief all the natural elements except fire, possibly because his life now ends. The musical recovery may exist as much within the narrative content as in the sentimental rhythm.

In *Fields of Wonder* (1947), the next most revealing of the lyrical volumes, Hughes disproves the critic's arbitrary and condescending claim: "His lyric poetry is no doubt of secondary importance in his work; yet, as usually happens with the minor work of great artists, this minor (lyric) poetry is high enough in quality and great enough in quantity to have sustained the reputation of a lesser poet."[21] Where the prescriptive critic favors the "social" verse, he accepts the distinction between lyric and rhetoric too readily.[22] But what generates the lyrical power in *Fields* conceals the real concern with community. Published originally in the *Christian Register* (May 1947), a twelve-line lyric titled "Birth" (*FW*, 9) highlights the artistic credo of Langston Hughes. Without directly addressing the social mission, as does the "cool poet" in "Motto" (*Montage*, 19; *SP*, 234),[23] it images the creative calling as stars, moon, and sun. Just as the lyric emotion subsides into the lyric process, so the pictorial frieze fades into the surge of dramatic action. Private feeling has become public deed. Where the social revolutionary seems displaced as the storyteller, he still speaks in undertone; indeed, he imposes his own signature and voice upon history:

stroke
Of lightning
In the night
Some mark to Make
some Word
to tell.

Indirectly, he confirms partially that "the imagination deals with feelings preferably wayward, congenially wild, and it wants to move them not into formulae but toward the state of value and purity for which Eliot's 'form' and 'pattern' are at once moving and still . . . The imagination makes nothing happen, but it lets things happen by removing obstacles of routine and providing a context of feeling from which they appear naturally to emerge."[24] The insight suits a literary theory derived in part from the school of art for art's sake toward the end of the nineteenth century in France, but as we have seen, to Langston Hughes the lyrical imagination was dynamic and fertile as well.

"Carolina Cabin" (FW, 9), a neglected poem about a Black couple later in love, displaces lyricism through the dramatic situation it presents. Viewed first as an imaginative landscape, the setting has hanging moss, holly, and "tall straight pine." The unfolding drama parallels the narrator's silent movement inward. Near the crackling fire and rare red wine, the storyteller hears good laughter. When he looks outward then, the gloomy world has

The winds of winter cold
As down the road
A wandering poet
Must roam.

Still, the plot resolves itself into reinforced laughter peacefully. Where love's old story recurs, people make a home. The poem provides an angle on post–World War II alienation in the United States. While the aesthetic world lures the speaker, he must return to realistic commitments eventually. So the diction carries both religious and secular connotations. The speaker, as a participant in the racial narrative implied, achieves the mythic dimensions of the Wandering Jew, for here he perceives the margins of myth and history. Far less dramatic and well-structured, "Old Sailor" (FW, 76-77) subordinates the lyric quality to a greater element of narrative.

> He has been
> Many places
> In ships
> That cross the sea,
> Has studied varied faces
> Has tasted mystery.

For twenty lines, a paralyzed mariner fancies women all over the world lamenting his absence. The tragicomic poem, indebted to Hughes' own days as a sailor during 1923-24, completes that career vicariously. So the literary work helps to close the frame on the historical life. In the first twelve lines the teller has "tasted" mysteries in oriental cities; with Bohemian joy and international sorrow, he has pursued the Dionysian urge.

> Now,
> Paralyzed
> He suns himself
> In charity's poor chair—
> And dreams.

But deteriorated finally into a dreamer, one who is unable to perform heroic deeds, he remembers sexual prowess and laughter from youth.

"Sailing Date" (FW, 87), similarly a revealing lyric about aging, tells in twenty-four lines and four stanzas the story of old mariners who face the fading years. Here are the twist, strangeness, and "bitter rage" of their lives. From youthful adventure ("salt sea water") the sailors have deteriorated to lushness ("whiskey shore"). As the decline marks broken dreams and imminent aging, the narration suggests their past.

> Go up the gangplank
> To the Nevermore—
> Perhaps—
> Or just another
> Trip.
>
> Why care?
> It's sailing date
> Their captain's
> There.

Experienced through a thousand storms, they have survived world wars; since the days when submarines once threatened them, they have mastered an ironic indifference.

Yet Hughes' subconscious allusions to Anglo-American verse seem to defer at first the telling citation of his own text, the racial self's brilliant revision of literary tradition for purposes of demonstration. For the tone, he draws heavily upon the traditional poetry of England and the United States, especially from the nineteenth century, though the sources, probably vague on his part, still merit original consideration.[25] In "O Captain! My Captain!"—a poem of biographical celebration—Whitman alludes to Abraham Lincoln (history) and to God (eternity). In "Crossing the Bar"—a verse, on the contrary, about the poetic facing of personal death—Tennyson allegorizes God (as the Pilot) alone. And Hughes himself celebrates Whitman in "Old Walt,"[26] a poem that reappeared appropriately in a chapbook called The Pilot. Whether regarding the president during the Civil War or the God beyond, Hughes' teller once more portrays events within historical time but projects himself beyond them imaginatively. While the implicit drama of history underscores Lincoln's death and Tennyson's life, probably without Hughes' conscious association, his lyrics of the sea emphasize the rituals of mourning and celebration, the products now of his own cited and elegiac release:

> Off the coast of Ireland
> As our ship passed by . . .
> Off the coast of England
> . . . an Indian merchantman
> Coming home. [WB, 78; SP, 53]

In "Trumpet Player: 52nd Street," one of the final poems in *Fields of Wonder*, as in "The Weary Blues," the dramatic performance completes the lyric impulse (*FW*, 93; *SP*, 114).[27] Here the quality implodes in the instrumental metaphor rather than in choral rhetoric. The player, in forty-four lines, distills jazz from "old desire" and hardship. Then, with the trumpet at his lips, he blows against and through the ambivalence toward acculturation, the paradox of racial identity. In the hair tamed down by the straightening process, he demonstrates more than style, for he would resemble whites whose hair is naturally tame. But he rejects socially what he has accepted artistically. The inner black light "glows" brilliantly through the process and "gleams" as if "jet [Black] were jet a crown"

What gives the image dramatic power has the lighted frieze playing counter to the persona's inner light and, indeed, to the elapsed time across which the song has been played as well as to the more transcendent Time, the symbolic goal of great music. But the music that sounds rhythmically reminds the reader that the temporal lapse between 1947 and 1989, or indeed any future date, is hardly an illusion by which speeding light tricks the eye. History and time, in challenge to lyrical experience, are real, though the narrator, who is distanced from them, concentrates on the trumpeter and the performance. Partly identifying with the sound and light, he relates the communion of the dramatic performance. In the arrestment of time, both auditory (sound) and visible (light), the player mixes "honey" with "liquid fire" (an oxymoron) in flowing and "burning" sweetness. Through the

dynamic performance he plays out the inert desire: in a scene
giving the illusion of permanence, he expresses "longing for the
moon" and "longing for the sea." When moonlight seems to
"flow" to the earth, he has resolved a paradox through the very
image, for if fire which produces light can "flow," thereby ap-
propriating to itself the quality of water, its contrasting element,
so the imagination might reverse or transform the posture from
which it has previously conceived the world and the universe.
Literary light and imagination may well be Black, and the black
light exorcises or releases any previous disillusion. When the final
repetend reinforces the dramatic performance, including the
frieze, the player sports his "one-button roll" jacket. In the convenient descent from the dramatic mode to the lyric one, the
narrator wonders about the trumpeter's motivation:

> Desire
> That is longing for the moon
> Where the moonlight's but a spotlight
> In his eyes,
> Desire
> That is longing for the sea
> . . . .
> But softly
> As the tune comes from his throat
> Trouble
> Mellows to a golden note.

Here is the great lyrical skill that we must reconsider on its
own terms. While the performance obscures the lyric form itself,
the latter subsides in the instrumental music. Here modernity
only appears to have displaced the pastoral world. Through rhetorical convention the soloist delivers the song to the chorus but
expects no answer. Though reaffirmations are silent in the poem,
they are yet implied. Thus, Langston Hughes, like Ezra Pound,
"found that he loved and praised only what Pindar and Horace
and Johnson and Whitman had loved and praised; perfection of

good order, the kinship of earth, the earth herself in her epi-
phanies of fertility, Nature, and culture, the paradises of earth
and the unearthly paradises that engender them, the dignity of
humankind and of the universe. Like his predecessor in choral,
he had also blamed what offered to harm or destroy what he
loved and praised, but he had spent too much time in blaming.
And the joy and celebration survived even that."[28]

Even the sensitive insight implies the illusions that Western
critics impose upon human history. At least three thousand years
before Pindar, the lyric in Africa must have made for the communal recitation during which the original humans listened to
history from the griot or storyteller. Today the lyric still marks
the ritual through which the self and society collectively reaffirm
community. Whether the poetic songs are vocal or instrumental,
the speakers merely displace or hide the common ritual they
inevitably share, for even the great lyric implies both a social
narrative and a dramatic event. What are the implications for
the reconsideration of a great poet? Langston Hughes made the
genre speak to a community again.

What brings about the brilliantly lyrical release here—as was
true in the autobiographies and in the intense poems on women,
and as surely will be found in the short fiction studied below—
is the way the protagonist dramatizes Black American creativity
in the face of social circumstance. In the allusion to Walt Whitman, the imaginative defender of human equality (yet the realistic advocate of racial separation) the white poet must keep
alive the memory of a cherished friend. And, like the player in
"Trumpet," Blacks distill an unfunny yet still comic hope of
better days, an apocalyptic song or vision, from the repressive
history that made them blow horns in the first place. The instrument as cultural emblem functions similarly to the horn of
the dead husband in "The Richer, the Poorer" by Dorothy West
and the guitar in "To Hell with Dying" by Alice Walker.[29] While
no particularly physical death has threatened the musicman in
this particular Hughes poem, the player has triumphed over dis-

illusion. Perhaps the moonlight that sets the scene for his blowing recalls the inner light of the ascendent woman in "Mother to Son." To Langston Hughes, lyrical beauty, whether physical or mental, defined itself through the temporary suspension of tragic death: "Black Maria passin' by / Leaves the sunrise in the sky.[30]

4

"OH, MIND OF MAN"
The Political Imagination

The reader who would most reconsider the lyrical imagination of Langston Hughes would probably dislike a fine poem such as "Madrid—1937." The formalist would argue for the universal autonomy and preeminence of verbal technique; the politician would likely propose an inflexible bond between literature and society. Neither would experience fully the literary richness of Langston Hughes, who rebelled inherently against a world where literary form displaces human life or, indeed, one where history displaces the importance of literary imagination. Though Hughes accepted explicitly the Marxist belief that history produces events and men—namely, the doctrine of Darwinian determinism—he believed as well that people determine their own fate, for he almost never minimized human will. When fiscal policies brought on the Great Depression of the United States in the 1930s and the subsequent aggression helped to provoke World War II, he still dreamed.

Hughes, believing in Marxism more discursively than naturally, is ambiguous on the subject. Facing the basic conceptions of materialism and colonialism, he seeks to bridge the rupture between the material form of the English language and the ironic need to materialize through this very language those ideas that seem at odds with a Euro-American perspective. To him, writing

becomes intellectual armament against colonialism throughout
the world. While *A New Song* (1938) illustrates his inability at
the age of thirty-six to analyze the complex flaws of liberal idealism, he is not naive about historical evil.

Hughes resists the Marxist tendency to repress conscience in
order to make history evolve according to some preordained pattern. *Jim Crow's Last Stand* (1943) shows his intransigence to
disillusion and his potential for self-recovery.

> Some folks think
> By burning books
> They burn freedom.
> . . . .
> Some folks think
> By lynching a Negro
> They lynch freedom.
>
> But freedom
> Stands up and laughs
> In their faces,
> And says,
>
> You'll *never kill me!*   ["Freedom," JC, 7]

Even in *Good Morning Revolution*, which lacks the structural and
chronological unity of the other published works, the tension
appears strongly. And when Hughes subsequently confronts the
social history of the years 1963-67, including the deaths of mar-
tyrs, and seems sometimes to abandon all hope, it is rarely for
long. Where such psychological complexities recur in *Ask Your
Mama* (1961), memory and human consciousness take shape
through words. Hughes provides, finally, not the mere reflection
of history but a brilliant and metaphoric code by which to read
the record profoundly. The narrative conscience does threaten
in *The Panther and the Lash* (1967) to regress into inevitable
brutality, as the counterpart to an even greater savagery imposed
upon the Black self:

Make a garland of Leontynes and Lenas
And hang it about your neck
    Like a lei,
Make a crown of Sammys, Sidneys, Harrys,
Plus Cassius Mohammed Ali Clay.
Put their laurels on your brow . . .
            ["Crowns and Garlands," *PL*, 6]

Yet, the collapse remains incomplete.

Langston Hughes gives verbal shape to the political and psychological struggle of humanity, particularly in American civilization. What is necessary for a reassessment of his political imagination is a careful reading of the developmental cycle that passes from direct didacticism (*A New Song*, 1938) through a more liberal and lyrical kind of political statement (*Jim Crow's Last Stand*, 1943) to a more symbolic rendition of the political world (*Good Morning Revolution*, 1925-53, collected 1973) and finally to a great psychological complexity (*Ask Your Mama*, 1961). Near the end of Hughes' life (*The Panther and the Lash*, 1967) his political imagination returns almost to the tone with which it began, though with some lyrical qualification.

What even Marxists could not read in history, Langston Hughes probably could have. Material form was the euphemism for greed, and though the Ice Age produced the fear and destitution that inspired such acquisitiveness, perhaps millions of years back—including the technological sublimation of it into "higher civilization"—the development had passed into Euro-American consciousness. Hughes knew well that people repress their instincts as well as their fears.

The past has been a mint
Of blood and sorrow
That must not be
True of tomorrow.[1]

Material fact condenses itself into psychic and collective memory, not only the tools of material forms; humans have the power to produce and change them. When the external inheritance of humanity has sometimes moved ahead, the internal one has nevertheless lagged behind it. To counterbalance the trend means to shape the ideas of freedom and spirit into some writings that rebel.

The imaginative writings of Hughes resist colonialism, and they hold suspect most defenses for the modern ethos, including industrial mechanization, military techniques, communications, and sophisticated finance. While some of the tenets suggest the political mythmaker—such as Franz Fanon—more than the poet, Hughes' imagination draws upon the indigenous rebellion of Africa, the transposed ideas of Western egalitarianism, and the fundamental changes in world power after 1945.[2]

Langston Hughes reattaches Western ideas to the political history of Africa, Asia, and the Pacific, for the modern empires were colonies of occupation which assured European rule over other peoples rather than colonization in the true sense. Through mechanization the Europeans improved armaments and business as well as health care and surplus capital. They conquered India through Britain and directed the decline of Ottoman power in the Balkans and the Mediterranean. In establishing a favorable trade balance with the advanced economies of the East, they infiltrated the first world. And until others generated their own industrial skills, the European power was overwhelming.

In response to historical materialism, Hughes provides an aesthetic one. When his creative words embody pan-African memory, they structure a paradigm for Blackness or racial consciousness, as in "Final Call":

> SEND (GOD FORBID—HE'S NOT DEAD LONG ENOUGH!)
> FOR LUMUMBA TO CRY "FREEDOM NOW!"
> SEND FOR LAFAYETTE AND TELL HIM, "HELP! HELP ME!
> SEND FOR DENMARK VESEY CRYING, "FREE!"
> FOR CINQUE SAYING, "RUN A NEW FLAG UP THE MAST."
> FOR OLD JOHN BROWN WHO KNEW SLAVERY COULDN'T LAST.
> [PL, 20-21]

Hughes translates racial beauty and ancestral heritage into verbal form, but the motivation is hardly the pure greed for objects and mere tools; for him the verbal structures are repositories for the soul and for celebration. Whereas for some others the motivation to use literary form may be material words in themselves, or the artistic externalization of physical need, Hughes uses it to suggest the fulfillment of the Dream.

Through the power of imagemaking he restores the geography of Africa and the impassioned response to beauty. In his literary world the pride of the contributions of all Blacks to world culture takes shape. Not some mere sublimation, or substitute gratification, his poems are political as well as cultural forms. Whatever the myopia of the Marxist position, his stories and plays, as well as his verses, make a difference in the real world. "Ideology . . . governs peoples' activities within economic and political practices; so the idea of a social revolution that is not accompanied by a revolution in ideology is a recipe for distaste; a recipe for a return to the structures that have been overthrown, brought about by the way people habitually and unconsciously act and relate."[3] Hughes translates the belief into the rhythms of tom-tom and jazz.[4]

> Perhaps
> You will remember
> John Brown
>
> John Brown
> Who took his gun
> Took twenty-one companions
> White and black . . .[5]

Not only protests against the most exclusive and aesthetic (as opposed to all) form of the West, his poems and essays are exemplary artifacts of the Black world. As a self-appreciation reconverted into a self-determination, they suggest imaginative power. From A New Song (1938) to Ask Your Mama (1961), Hughes must develop an effective critique of liberal Marxism.

But he can do so only intuitively, for he engages in discursive thought only rarely. Though Marxism argues for a demonstrable revolution in human history, liberalism holds for good will, for the potential redemption of fellows through enlightenment, and for interracial as well as international brotherhood. Whereas Marxism emphasizes self-interest and inevitable conflict, liberalism proposes altruism instead. Marxism clarifies the certainty of barbaric conflict; liberalism claims transcendence for the soul. Liberalism, itself grounded in humane reason, emerges from the Enlightenment, which Marxism seeks to overthrow.

What we reconsider here is an implicit assumption almost none of the voluminous scholarship on Hughes focuses on it explicitly. Throughout his life Hughes demonstrated an inherent distrust of both liberal idealism and Marxist determinism. As the voice of ego or sincere compromise, his political imagination mediates between biological death and moral compulsion. One example is a poem about political prisoners. In "Chant for Tom Mooney" (NS, 14-15) the speaker proposes the materiality of ideas as opposed to that of artifacts. The underlying paradigm suits Africa as well as China. The speaker says about Mooney, the prisoner whose release was called for in the Communist platform in 1936,

> Of course, the man with the title of governor
> Will be forgotten then
> On the scrap heap of time—
> . . . .
> But remembered forever will be the name . . .

Hughes' ambivalence toward materialism reappears in "Lynching Song," another of the more telling examples from A New Song. Here the wordplay on the literal and metaphorical levels provokes irony in penetrative suggestiveness. When the white lynchers pull the rope on the Black victim higher, they live on as he dies. But in the sarcastic "pull it boys," the narrator's diction suggests the perversion derived from the lynchers' own failure to achieve humane manhood either before or after the ritualistic murder. In attacking the Black victim physically, the lynchers emasculate themselves figuratively. *"The white folks die / What do you mean— / The white folks die?"* Though the hangmen read history deterministically, the narrator reads it morally; while they view only the victim's death, he perceives their own. Despite the claims of liberal Marxism, the speaker has his doubts about its goodwill, for here the cynical tone displaces the Messianic one that often appears in Hughes' work.

When the penetrative imagination overcomes the moral or the receptive one, as in the example of "Madrid—1937," a contemporary poem about the Spanish Civil War (GMR, 105-6), the rhetoric intervenes in the dramatic situation, reasserting the priority of conscience. The speaker invites others to share in his verbal simulation of the flamenco song, the thrust in the bullfight, the fascist's assault on the self-determined country. Whereas the described paintings of Goya (1746-1829), Velasquez (1599-1660), and Murillo (1617-82) dignified Spain during earlier times, the biological principle intervenes now. So piercing forms (bombs, planes, bullets, and knives) displace the great art as well as literature from the age of Cervantes. Yet an inherent contradiction about Western civilization appears. The age of exploration concealed ethnocentricity and exploitation beneath the polished artifacts. Euro-American art has barbaric roots in the past, including those that even Hughes himself partly overlooked, for artifacts, as enduring inspirations, help perpetuate nevertheless an image of beauty paid for in sacrifice and blood. Bullfights, paintings, and books are therefore not the imitations of men in action; they are, rather, the continuous actions of men.[6]

Despite its stock devices and the thematic overkill, the title poem in *A New Song* is nearly as fine.[7] In a fifty-seven-line exhortation the speaker invokes response from the audience yet delays it. He hones language into a dynamic act, suggesting the Black folk sermon. For an imaginative moment the poem freezes the material sequences of history, as the verse reasserts the moral as well as the social will. Whereas the Marxist proposes the causality behind events, this narrator distills the significance from

the 1930s. Inevitably bound to the past, he frees himself from
it partly.

> I speak in the name of the black millions
> Awakening to action
> Let all others keep silent a moment.
> I have this word to bring
> This song to sing.

The words embody masterful skill in colloquial and folk idiom.
The historical sequences are formulaic. The verse, tracing events
from slavery on through Jim Crow segregation, chronicles the
emasculation of Black men and the rape of Black women.
Through the tales of lynching and tar-and-feathering, it reveals
historical oppression. Black art reduces itself consequently to
sublimation: "And only in the sorrow songs / Relief was found."
But even the immaterial spirituals have prepared for dynamic
poetry a century later:

> New words are formed,
> Bitter with the past
> But sweet
> With the dream
> Tense,
> Unyielding
> Strong and sure,
> They sweep the earth—

A *New Song* poses all the political complications Hughes faced
for over thirty years. Where do the proletarian cliché and the
personal signature divide? Can white and Black workers form a
workers' coalition on any continent where those of African and
Asian ancestry have been enslaved and colonized? Whatever the
disclaimers of the formalist, and whatever those of the poet, who
himself disavows any interest in critical theories or such questions
(Hughes said he never thought about poetry too seriously), he
faces at once his art and his social world. And several tenets for
the political imagination emerge. At the interface of history

(event) and myth (pattern), that imagination illuminates the Scottsboro affair in 1931. While revealing the discrepancy between the American ideal and the real world, it sets into relief the ever expanding paradigm of world injustice and the necessary resistance to it.

In *Jim Crow's Last Stand* (1943) materialism corrupts the world. "Ballad of the Landlord" presents a tenant who refuses to pay his rent.[8] Because the roof of the building he lives in needs repairs (first stanza) and the steps are broken (second stanza), resistance on his part seems justified. When he refuses (in the third stanza) to pay ten dollars until the house is fixed, the landlord threatens him with eviction and bodily harm, to which the tenant responds (the fourth and fifth stanzas):

> What? You gonna get eviction orders?
> You gonna cut off my heat?
> You gonna take my furniture and
> Throw it in the street?
>
> Um-huh! You talking high and mighty.
> Talk on—till you get through.
> You ain't gonna be able to say a word
> If I land my fist on you.

Following the fifth stanza's reversal of the poem's general thrust— the narrator promising physical reciprocity to the landlord—the proprietor directs his rhetoric outward to the police, who have heard about the tenant's "subversive" activities: *"He's tryin to ruin the government / And overturn the land!"* The tenant is jailed in an iron cell at the precinct station, and a newspaper headline reads:

> Man Threatens Landlord
> Tenant Held No Bail
> Judge Gives Negro 90 Days In County Jail

As auditory images (whistle, bell) contribute to an expressionistic mood, the speaker clarifies the way the media distort dramatic as well as social truth into propaganda. Whether abroad or at home, words may serve either to liberate victims or to enslave them. Yet the political posture must not obscure literary experimentation. When Langston Hughes' bluesy wit blossoms fully, he achieves a stream of consciousness and an effective sweep in dramatic expression as well as psychological association. Where the newspaper headlines displace the political narrative, the speaker has told the story through the visual flash.

In "Note on Commercial Theater" the skillful performance derives from the dramatic reversal, moving as it does from narrated history to the prophetic vision expressed through Black American idiom: "Yep, you done taken my blues and gone."[9] The "you," as the corrupter of art and the Dream, has made the blues and Black heritage stereotypical. The distorted forms appear on Broadway and in symphonies that "don't sound like me." The speaker shifts in midstanza from rhetorical protest to lyrical introspection:

> But someday somebody'll
> Stand up and talk about me,
> And write about me—
> Black and beautiful—
> And sing about me,
> And put on plays about me!

With a masterful blend of humor and confidence, the speaker reaffirms his self-determination: "I reckon it'll be / Me myself! / It'll be me."

The second movement in *Jim Crow's Last Stand*, with its motif of death and anger, prepares for the spiritual recovery of the Black self within political history as well as within modern consciousness. In the dramatic ballad "Blue Bayou" (*JC*, 10; *SP*, 170) Old Greeley becomes involved sexually with Lou, the Black narrator's lover and perhaps his wife.

> I went walkin'
> By de blue bayou

And I saw de sun go down.

. . . .

And I saw de sun go down,
  Down,
    Down!
Lawd, I saw de sun go down!

Although the lynchers believe that only a physical death has happened, the speaker reads a spiritual one as well. From the beginning, his walk has suggested a pilgrimage that resists the passing of time. When the biological world gives way to the moral one, the lynchers again emerge as being as dead as the lynched man. The skillful word acrostic on death, "I saw de sun go down," applies alike to the victimizer and the victim.[10] From top left to bottom right, for example, the poem reads "And Down, Down! down!" but from right top to bottom left the piece says "go down, Down, Lawd," hence redeeming Death.

In "The Bitter River" (JC, 13) the political imagination fails to distill human meaning from despair. Through anaphora and litany—"There is a bitter river. . . . There is . . . ,"—the poem renders social injustice faithfully. Yet the skill in dramatic rhetoric and in narrative posture facilitates an irony. Through the feigned guise of the liberal and the political accuser who intrudes into the narrative plot ("Disrupter," "Agitator! / Trouble Maker"), the speaker doubts the truthfulness of Emersonian self-reliance. For the speaker in the imaginative world, as for Langston Hughes in the historical and real one, the paradox is finally insoluble. Concentration on only the political landscape of the lynched boys and on the unreflected light would confine the poet to the depiction of the id or to that of people at their worst. An emphasis on form alone would mean the naive neglect of the social and human prices to be paid. The political imagination partly contradicts its own existence so long as the social poet must emphasize survival, and yet the political mission must nearly always be central in an imperfect world. Gwendolyn Brooks would write about Langston Hughes that he

Holds horticulture
In the eye of the vulture
Infirm profession.
In mud and blood and sudden death—
In the breath of the holocaust he
Is helmsman, hatchet, headlight.
See
One restless in the exotic time! and ever,
Till the air is cured of its fever.[11]

Whereas the poetic speaker in "The Negro Speaks of Rivers" (1921) was redeemed through water, the "you" in "Bitter River" "spits" in "the face" of the dream. The music and water hardly reflect light now but do image evil in the natural world. Sensitive to the liberal prescription for goodwill and redemptive education, few have dared quote Hughes here:

I have drunk at the river too long
Dreamer of dreams to be broken
Builder of hopes to be smashed
Loser from an empty pocket
Of my mere cash
Bitter bearer of burdens.

Despite countermovements toward despair and chaos, the final recovery in *Jim Crow's Last Stand* appears through the metaphors of fight and Africa. Rather than forming mere themes, the images shape themselves into complexes of emotion and meaning balancing themselves in the unconscious. Here the poet reappropriates to himself the figurative power of the ancient and ancestral image; indeed, he superbly diverts the penetrative overtones of colonization and Nazi militarism into the highest hopes for human community.

"To Captain Mulzac (Negro Skipper of the *Booker T. Washington*)," (*JC*, 16-18) for example, has vision and figurative precision as well as stylistic grace. The speaker expands the dramatic situation of a battleship during World War II into the symbolic

scope of worldwide oppression and the relentless quest for freedom. As in the earlier poem "Oppression" (*FW*, 112), sorrow
follows hope. What reads as political allegory deepens into the
cataclysmic threat for which moral cleansing remains impotent.
When the allusion to biblical pilgrimage combines with the metaphor of slavery, the symbolic complexes are rich:

Dangerous
Are the Western waters now
And all the waters of the World
Somehow,
Again mankind has lost its course,
Been driven off its way,
Down paths of death and darkness
Gone astray—

The controlled narrative signifies the speaker as pilot and
fighter as well as guard. While he protests the social and historical
past—"those, too, who for so long / Could not call their house,
their house / Nor their land, their land"—the maritime journey
has deeper implications. Hughes rewords a complex figure for
which the source extends at least from Donne through Tennyson
to Yeats. With chart and compass, the speaker "guards the harbor" or holds back chaos. The poet or guard diverts the listener
to a "brighter day." Throughout the poem, within its psychological depth, the humane will reasserts itself over barbarism or
over the biological destruction potentially residing in the sea.
Though the second and third parts favor didacticism over such
symbolic complexity, the third sets the tone for what follows.
Where poetic vision has served well, political discourse suggests
ineffectualness. What the speaker says discursively now the brilliant opening has already revealed even more skillfully: those
without self-determination and power are alone. The narrator
asserts the existence of progress, but moral regression characterizes Italy and Japan as well as Germany during the period; fascism
embodies social injustice in material form. And even before then,
Langston Hughes "could not forget about segregation, even if he

was removed from it in Carmel Valley, where he wrote 'Daybreak
in Alabama,' 'Sunset in Dixie,' 'Merry Go Round,' and 'Southern
Negro Speaks.' The latter, published that October in *Opportunity*,
expressed his ambivalence about America's willingness to fight
a war to defend European democracy when racial equality had
not been achieved at home. It was the first half of a dozen of
his poems on that theme during the war years. Some would appear
later in *Jim Crow's Last Stand*."[12]

"How About It Dixie?" (*JC*, 9) uses irony as a device to recover
from personal doubt.

> Looks like by now
> Folks ought to know
> It's hard to beat Hitler
> Protecting Jim Crow

The speaker points out the need for a single standard of political
ethics. When the president's Four Freedoms appeal to the narrator, he wants them for himself. Needless exposition underscores
the caustic irony, yet the speaker creates the metaphor of beauty
("those Freedoms") that resists oppression.

The political imagination in *Jim Crow's Last Stand* restores
itself through human memory and sacrifice as well as moral power.
"October 16" (*JC*, 14), for example, indicates the degree to which
the 1930s would continue to shape Hughes' view of the world.

> Perhaps today
> You will remember John Brown.
>
> John Brown
> Who took his gun,
> Took twenty-one companions
> White and black,
> Went to shoot your way to freedom
> Where two rivers meet.

The rhetorical invocation gives way in turn to echo and exhortation. What distinguished Brown was the coherent vision of the

rebellion he carried out in American history. When he stood at Harper's Ferry in 1859, the year in which he invaded a federal arsenal and consequently lost his life, his vision seemed almost lyrical.

It is appropriate that the narrator of *Jim Crow's Last Stand* recovers from bitterness either temporarily through such lyricism or through cryptic as well as humorous speech. "Daybreak in Alabama," for instance, converts political history into personal and racial idiom. Precisely this rupture between worlds, between Earth and Paradise Regained, makes for lyric power. Even the leftist clichés ("black hands and brown and yellow hands") displace themselves into the romantic vision. One day the speaker would like to be a composer and write about daybreak in Alabama. Into the composition he would write the "purtiest songs," which rise from the ground "like a swamp mist" or fall from heaven "like soft dew." When the third and fourth sections complete the fantasy, tall trees and pine needles appear in the work. The musical composition seems more like a painting because the images are so vivid. In the imagined world of interracial harmony, long necks and poppy-colored faces will eventually blend with "big brown arms." Later, the movements of the poem culminate in the narrator's sexual union with nature: "Touching everybody with kind fingers / Touching each other natural as dew."[13]

At first the emblem of nature and the psychological depth would seem to exclude political substance from the outstanding lyric. Though Alabama was a crucial state to southern slavery, the fact merits only passing attention or allusion here. Nevertheless, "Daybreak" signifies Black American freedom, the meaning residing in the onomatopoeic rise and fall ("When I get to be a composer I'm gonna write me some music") as well as in the patterns of reversal and unfinished struggle.[14] Two hidden clues, one textual and the other psychological, reveal that politics still subsists in the lyric. Though the revised text in *Selected Poems* (1959) would say "Get to be a composer," an earlier draft read "Get to be a *colored* composer" (my italics). When the political climate changed, so did the diction of the poet. Whatever the suggestions of supposedly neutral art, such creativity refers to the historical world necessarily though obliquely. The poetic narrator envisions a musical composition, itself a fantasy, while the fantasized poem is itself a dream about a dream. Insofar as the fantasy in the lyrical narrative reminds us of this dream within a dream, it draws attention to the fact that the poem itself is a fiction as well. Yet even such subtle disclosure reminds us that history continues its course dynamically, on the outside beyond both dreams. Eventually the vision of an Alabama paradise must fade back to World War II, and, indeed (given the posthumous reprinting of the poem in 1967), back to the very real riots in Selma and Birmingham.

The title poem, as part of the final movement in *Jim Crow's Last Stand*, lacks polish and complexity of image. Yet though the fluency ranks well below that of Hughes' finest verse, the quickness of expression does suggest the subtle advance in his technical development, his progress from a lyric emphasizing external landscape to a more reflective and unified consciousness. The tendency becomes particularly clear in the writings collected posthumously in *Good Morning Revolution*.[15] When Hughes transcends the party line, as in "Madrid—1937," he crafts a brilliant poem. This previously unpublished verse, which was inscribed "Langston" to Arthur P. Spingarn and deposited in the collection at Howard University, recounts the story implied in the title.

Damaged by artillery shells, many of the clocks in Madrid are still. Franco's troops assault The loyalist forces, yet the battle is only signified. What concerns the speaker is the stream of consciousness that reconstitutes history into psychological and moral form.

> Time's end and throw-back
> Birth of darkness
> Years of light reduced:
> The ever-minus of the brute
> The nothingness of barren land
> And stone and metal . . .   [GMR, 104]

To perform the rite of the story, the narrator urges the reader to extinguish light and stop time. While humanity mocks its own potential to build and grow, the rhetorical address shapes itself into urban apostrophe: "Time's end and throw-back." When the Spanish Civil War intrudes upon the poetic imagination, the speaker knows that even humane forms revert to instinct, "Years of light reduced."

Where human civilization itself stands still, bombs and planes represent the penetrative rape of conscience. But rhetorical address—"Oh, Mind of Man!"—seeks to replace instinct and material achievement with dynamic imagination. From the focus on fire, oil, and gas, as well as on electricity, the poet shifts to the evolution of human time itself. Where the sundial marks the frieze of the literary imagination against fascist history, the primal purpose clarifies itself: "So long to struggle upward out of darkness / To a measurement of time / And now . . . " Outside the frozen sequence and still within historical time, brainless killers subvert humane possibility to atrocity in the Guadarrama hills. Here is the background of "stopped clocks in towers," in the way sequential history threatens imaginative poetry, for each form seeks to externalize a different side of the human psyche. While war aims to materialize the culture for the purposes of physical acquisition, poetry intends to objectify humane aspiration. Langston Hughes articulates the inadequacy of a materialistic aesthetic in which objects, such as the books back in his childhood or land as the aim of conquest, usurp the rightful place of humanity. Even at the close, the rhetorical overkill infuses the dramatic situation with symbolic images that confront chaos: "*To all the killers of man's dreams, Madrid cries No!*" (GMR, 106). Where the verbal form presents metal shells (piercing power) and stopped clocks, it opposes the bombed-out lights once more. While the narrator says "no" to regressive civilization, the broken clocks signify "timeless midnight."

"Concerning 'Goodbye Christ' " (Jan. 1, 1941; GMR, 36-37) and "My Adventures as a Social Poet" (GMR, 135-43; *Phylon*, Fall 1947) confirm Hughes' ambivalence about such a political imagination. "Goodbye Christ" (*Negro Worker*, Nov.-Dec. 1932) had provoked controversy, especially from bigots who blamed the leftist tone more easily than their own prejudice. Hughes had intended to shock people into the discovery or their religious hypocrisy. Having completed a tour of the United States in 1931, he had seen suffrage denied to Blacks generally. He had met with the Scottsboro boys, but many other Blacks had been intimidated into silence. Then he crossed the river by ferry, the Blacks waited in line for all whites to pass ahead of them. He saw and regretted the unemployment and hunger in the great urban centers. Even in Black colleges and universities, as well as in restaurants, he had found segregation still alive and well.

When the Temple of the Four Square Gospel, a group led by Aimee McPherson, resurrected the poem in 1941, he was too apologetic about it all. Advanced then from the radical at the age of twenty to the conservative at the age of forty, he urged new readers to ignore "Goodbye Christ," which supposedly re-flected his views no longer:

> I would not now use such a technique of approach since I feel that a mere poem is quite unable to compete in power to shock with the current horrors of war and oppression abroad in the greater part of the world. I have never been a member of the communist party. Furthermore, I have come to believe that no system of ethics, religion, morals or government is of permanent value which does not first *start with and change the human heart*. Mortal frailty, greed, and error, know no boundary lines. The *explosives* of war do not care whose *hands* fashion them. Certainly, both *Marxists* and *Christians* can be cruel. Would that Christ came back to save us all. We do not know how to save ourselves. [GMR, 135; my emphasis]

What distinguishes the passage is the turn from material form to moral substance. To Hughes, both Marxism and Darwinism had repressed the compassionate self at least in part, though the speaker understands such history painfully.

Even when Hughes believed he had failed, his poetic forms provoked responses in the political world. "My Adventures as a Social Poet" says that the poets who write about love, roses, and moonlight, sunset and snow, probably live quiet lives. Skeptical about beauty and lyricism,[16] the speaker distrusts aesthetic distance ("ivory towers") as well as mystification. While such poetry excites the police rarely, the social kind prompts deep interest immediately. In their concern for poverty and injustice, the poets Placido and Lorca were killed in ways that disturbed Hughes greatly. Now harassed by social groups himself, he continues to see through superficial patriotism. But unable to write "*exclusively* [my emphasis] about roses and moonlight," he portrays the terror of the Klan which confronts the Black community so forcefully:

> They took me out
> To some lonesome place.
> They said, "Do you believe
> In the great white race?   ["Ku Klux," *SP*, 163]

Whatever the debatable claims for the distinction of *Fine Clothes to the Jew* and *Good Morning Revolution*, the political imagination achieves its most brilliant expression in *Ask Your Mama* (1961).[17] Here the imagination extends to the very limits of narrative consciousness.

> GOT THERE! YES, I MADE IT!
> NAME IN THE PAPERS EVERYDAY!
> FAMOUS—THE HARD WAY
> FROM NOBODY AND NOTHING TO WHERE I AM
> THEY KNOW ME, TOO, DOWNTOWN,
> ALL ACROSS THE COUNTRY, EUROPE—
> ME WHO USED TO BE NOBODY,
> NOTHING BUT ANOTHER SHADOW
> IN THE QUARTER OF THE NEGROES,
> NOW A NAME! MY NAME—A NAME!
>   ["Horn of Plenty," *AYM*, 43]

Like Robert Hayden's *Middle Passage* and Gwendolyn Brooks's *In the Mecca, Ask Your Mama* reconstitutes racial and modern awareness. Profound in scope and reach, it calls into question the boundaries between poetry and music as well as those between literature and politics. The work, in other words, signifies a human structure that transcends easy formulas.

SINGERS
SINGERS LIKE O—
SINGERS LIKE ODETTA—AND THAT STATUE
ON BEDLOE'S ISLAND MANAGED BY SOL HUROK
DANCERS BOJANGLES LATE LAMENTED
. . . .
JAZZERS DUKE AND DIZZY ERIC DOLPHY
MILES AND ELLA AND MISS NINA
STRAYHORN HID BACKSTAGE WITH LUTHER
DO YOU READ MUSIC? AND LOUIS SAYING
NOT ENOUGH TO HURT MY PLAYING
. . . .
BONDS AND STILL AND MARGARET STILL
GLOBAL TROTTERS BASEBALL BATTERS
JACKIE WILLIE CAMPANELLA
FOOTBALL PLAYERS LEATHER PUNCHERS
UNFORGOTTEN JOES AND SUGAR RAYS
WHO BREAK AWAY LIKE COMETS . . .   [AYM, 41-42]

Here Langston Hughes expresses the yearning toward self-fulfillment and the perfect poem, yet the impossibility of ever grasping them through genres and social laws. In "Cultural Exchange" he revives many of his most powerful themes.[18]

IN THE QUARTER OF THE NEGROES
WHERE THE DOORS ARE DOORS OF PAPER
DUST OF DINGY ATOMS
BLOWS A SCRATCHY SOUND
AMORPHOUS JACK-O-LANTERNS CAPER

AND THE WIND WONT WAIT FOR MIDNIGHT
FOR FUN TO BLOW DOORS DOWN.

The speaker, often apparently Christian, alludes perhaps to voodoo a bit.

IN THE POT BEHIND THE PAPER DOORS
ON THE OLD IRON STOVE WHAT'S COOKING?
WHATS SMELLING, LEONTYNE?
LEIDER, LOVELY LEIDER
AND A LEAF OF COLLARD GREEN
LOVELY LEIDER, LEONTYNE.

Whatever the church, the worshipers have sorrows. They face either assimilation and colonization on the one hand or militancy and surrealistic anger on the other. Focusing inward to ideas and contexts yet outward from them as well, the narrator advances to the century beyond the Underground Railroad, founded to further the abolition of slavery. Whatever the achievements of the talented tenth, the intellectually elite and privileged, the remaining scars of race extend across the performing arts. Here freedom materializes:

BY THE RIVER AND THE RAILROAD
WITH FLUID FAR-OFF GOING
BOUNDARIES BIND UNBINDING
A WHIRL OF WHISTLES BLOWING.
NO TRAINS OR STEAMBOAT'S GOING—
YET LEONTYNE'S UNPACKING.

To express intellectual depth, the poet draws brilliantly upon numerous techniques, several of them original as well as experimental. In finishing the patterns of death and recovery, the narrator flashes in and out of the child's consciousness, yet speaks then from the adult's:

YOU KNOW, RIGHT AT CHRISTMAS
THEY ASKED ME IF MY BLACKNESS,

WOULD IT RUB OFF?
I SAID ASK YOUR MAMA.

In making the verbal script face the marginalia, or the directions
for the musical background, he sets verbal and iconographic language (poem) against even more temporal language (music). The
intriguing arrangement allows the music and words to read the
same or to contradict each other in the collective formation of
irony. The strategy also achieves a reversal of mood.

Even these observations hardly exhaust the strategies in this
text, for Hughes expends nearly all he has ever learned here. His
narrator turns now from the wild leaps into fantasy to the polemical reversal of stereotype.

WHITE SHARECROPPERS WORK THE BLACK PLANTATIONS
AND COLORED CHILDREN HAVE WHITE MAMMIES:
    MAMMY FAUBUS
    MAMMY EASTLAND
    MAMMY WALLACE . . .

The speaker is refering to the white politicians and southern
segregationists of the period, but the extrinsic concerns subsume
themselves early into cosmic imagery and allegory as well as
paradox. Because the radical meanings often hide themselves
below the surface, the book appears safe and symphonic. My
claim for its excellence and plea for reconsideration rest upon
the dialectic between the verbal and musical languages. While
the narrator discusses the political militancy of Nkrumah, the
West African liberator, the musical accompaniment plays blues
and leider in the first two movements. The first movement implies bold aggression; the second suggests artistic retreat. When
the speaker's words tell about slavery angrily, "IN THE QUARTER
OF THE NEGROES," the two languages effectively mirror each
other. Even while the verbal plot exposes fantasy and stereotype,
the musical plot still reads "when the saints come marching in."

For the most part, the third and fourth movements of the
volume represent accommodation between the languages. As a

testimony to the unique structure, it is virtually impossible to recreate the scenes on the scholarly page. When the narrator describes apocalypse, the music reads "Saints." While he ridicules political regression, a discordant flute blows from the narrative stage. The speaker pantomimes the white myth that Blacks sing well, but the orchestra plays the spirituals well anyway. When the narrator remembers the Underground Railroad nobly, the drummer beats out the Battle Hymn of the Republic forcefully. As the storyteller portrays Niagara Falls in winter, the musicians sound the chorus of death, though the poet tells about urban and racial progress in general. The orchestra hesitates in the playing, and during the narrator's presentation of lynching the music retards itself. While the speaker proclaims the certainty of Black American victory in the social struggle, the music "dies" ironically. When the narrator suggests Christian doubt, the instrumentalists respond in kind. Despite racial embarrassment on the part of so many personae, the personified flute "calls."

In the final movement the narrator accepts the transformation of the social world into the imaginative one. Through irony and aspiration, sorrow converts itself into the flute. The folk "dozens"—the child's game of one-upsmanship—fades into the figurine. However much jazz and blues may pass from the poetic narrative, they pervade Western music. The pan-African source reveals itself still in the drums and dance as well as in the human heartbeat.

What Hughes provides involves the process of creativity itself; it includes the condensation of politics and the transformation of it into new shapes. Though political repression seems to carry more human weight than cadences in music, the pan-African naiveté of Sedar Senghor, president of Senegal, and of Martin Luther King, Jr., a leader for Civil Rights in the United States, seems to promise only an ethereal climax for the world history to come after them. But the poem, like their idealistic acts, resists any death for the spirit forged in the African diaspora. While the deeds by political luminaries such as Kwame Nkrumah, Jomo Kenyatta, and Ralph Bunche ("who break away like comets") belie any real gains for the masses, and though the figures merge into the musical tapestry finally, the poetic drama transcends them. "Cultural Exchange" distills political history into cosmic imagery as well as into the quest for human space. While ideas are only the intellectual forms of materialistic history, the interpretive self ("for a moment I wondered") reappears at intervals within historical sequences ("come what may Langston Hughes").

Without a narrative sequence at the center, the poem depends on the unity that consciousness imposes upon psychological association. From the early nineteenth century, the narrative seemingly leaps across vast segments of chronological history. Without discursive transitions, it advances to the "dust of dingy atoms" and the nuclear age. And the wind at the door implies the impulse that humanity has sublimated into more "civil" forms since World War II. Even children's games on Halloween hint the rematerialization of the biological past and the present rituals that seek subtly to exorcise terror. While instinct diverts the speaker to an invocation of the river, the image of eternity and spiritual restoration, social ambition presses him toward the railroad. Though technology displaces the urge toward poetic narrative, the creative form shaped through memory, it degrades the first world as much as it impoverishes humanity: "THERE FORBID US TO REMEMBER, / COMES AN AFRICAN IN MID-DECEMBER / SENT BY THE STATE DEPARTMENT / AMONG THE SHACKS TO MEET THE BLACKS". Despite the ambivalent examples of Leontyne Price and Sammy Davis, Jr., for whom racial assimilation carries a personal price, "come what may Langston Hughes."

In "Shades of Pigmeat," one of the last sections in *Ask Your Mama* (18-21), the political imagination expresses itself through the aging narrator. Whatever the peripheral concerns, Hughes at the age of fifty-eight preoccupies himself with the effects of time. Attentive to the greater world, the narrator knows that the days of Premier Downing and General Bourse (to name two colonial politicians) are numbered. The well-chosen allusions build to a crescendo in the passing of time. Adam Clayton Powell,

Jr., the preacher and politician, had risen to prominence in Harlem during 1938, and by 1945 Mahalia Jackson had become renowned for the song "Move On Up a Little Higher." Having already influenced Huddie "Leadbelly" Ledbetter, a folksinger born in 1885, Blind Lemon Jefferson had been one of the greatest blues singers. But he had still frozen to death during a Chicago snowstorm in 1930.[19] When the narrator alludes to Harriet Tubman, a fugitive slave and leader of the Underground Railroad as early as 1849, the ice imagery deepens:

> Cold Niagara
> Ghostly Monument of Winter
> To A Board That Once Passed Over
> With A Woman With Two Pistols
> On A Train That Lost No Passengers
> On The Line Whose Route Was Freedom

While the references and allusions occur out of chronological order, they reflect the imagination's unique way of perceiving them. History moves in sequence, but epic moves simultaneously from the tale's middle back to the beginning and forward to the end.

"Blues in Stereo" and "Horn of Plenty" profit from mythical as well as psychological space. The speaker parodies Thanksgiving in a honed retort: "I thought I heard the Horn of Plenty Blowing . . . But / . . . Lord . . . My T.V. Keeps on Snowing." The style develops deftly into engaging wit:

> Unforgotten Joes and Sugar Rays
> Who Break Away Like Comets
> From Lesser Stars In Orbit
> To Move out to St. Albans
> Where the grass is greener . . .

Though the passage narrates appropriately the stories of leading sports figures—Jackie Robinson, Willie Mays, Roy Campanella—the ending has a highly unexpected twist: all the athletes portrayed lived in the United States, but St. Albans (a New York

City suburb, is a municipal borough in southeast England. In fine fashion the narrator associates physical place with mental space. While he notes the need for better schools and opportunities elsewhere, the threats to self-appreciation do pose dangers. The middle-class Black will never close the political distance between races. Despite any acceptance of the Emersonian ideal of self-reliance on his or her part, a mainstream reputation remains insecure for those who must seek it so constantly without relief. Whatever the futile quest for distinction on European grounds (St. Albans), racial slights will impede the efforts and will keep Blacks honest despite themselves: "YET THEY ASKED ME OUT ON MY PATIO / WHERE DID I GET MY MONEY!"

The space between the Black narrator and the white neighbors widens. In apparently polite talk, the acquaintances ask the speaker why Richard Wright lived in Paris for so long and why Wright did not die decently in Harlem. Yet Wright's biographical roots, leading back to Chicago, Memphis, and Biloxi, almost certainly never led to Harlem. What except race connects the author and the place in their minds? The liberal neighbors have concealed a deep prejudice repressed even from themselves, for they believe that Richard Wright, too, should have stayed in his place and lived somewhere else.

For Langston Hughes, after thirty years, the psychological depth underscores the intuitive critique of liberalism as well as Marxism. When race and the iconography of race assume material forms in the society, even economic equality cannot assure human community. The athletes and others have not closed the distance between the white neighbors and themselves yet have alienated themselves from the Black community. The space in "Horn of Plenty" materializes finally as the no-man's-land in "Passing" (*Phylon*, Spring 1950); there the Black protagonist becomes "white" for good. Though liberalism allows for material changes in the human community, the philosophy can modify neither racial thought nor the tone in human relations.

In "Gospel Cha-Cha" and "Is It True" the compulsion toward truth resists this alienation. While allusions to African deities set the tone, Toussaint L'Overture (the nineteenth-century revolutionary) sharpens into focus. With the dual perspective on myth and history, the speaker exposes religious charlatans. In an ironic play upon continued persecution under Christianity, he proposes an end to the ritual:

> When I got to Calvary
> Up there on that Hill
> Already There Was Three
> And one, yes, One
> Was Black As Me.   ["Gospel," AYM, 52]

The imagery of crucifixion reverts to that of Christmas. The immaterial shadow gives way to more tangible light and the implied silence to sound.

> FROM THE SHADOWS OF THE QUARTER
> SHOUTS ARE WHISPERS CARRYING
> TO THE FARTHEST CORNERS SOMETIMES
> OF THE NOW KNOWN WORLD
> UNDECIPHERED UNPASSED
> IN TONGUES UNANALYZED UNECHOED
> UNTAKEN DOWN ON TAPE—   ["Is It True," AYM, 55]

Here Langston Hughes expresses the contour of the repressed Western subconscious.[20]

In the title poem (AYM, 61-65) he exposes the repressed memory of the Black middle class instead. While Porgy and Bess provides economic opportunity for the performers who participate, pan-Africanism unites the Americas, Africa, and Harlem as well as the Caribbean. Black students wear horn-rimmed glasses while taking six classes at the Sorbonne. Though they forsake Judaeo-Christian sacrifice for a more expedient and liberal idealism, how deep is the commitment: "WHY RIDE A MULE OR DONKEY / WHEN THERE'S A UNICORN?" Though they have apparently transcended racial identity, the narrator's view (expressed as a child's curiosity once more) looks back to the African diaspora and to the cottonfields of the southern United States. Fred-

erick Douglass, John Brown, and Sojourner Truth (all nineteenth-century abolitionists) come to the fore now. Within both
temporal and spatial frames, the speaker tells the story of Sojourner, who bared her breasts publicly in order to prove that
she was indeed a woman. She had said about her children:

> I look at the Stars
> And they *wonder* where I Be
> And I *wonder* where they be
> Stars at Stars, Stars . . . [My emphasis]
>   ["Bird in Orbit," AYM, 72]

The imagery of sight ("look") prepares for that of aspiration
("stars"), yet the external concern gives way to romantic introspection ("wonder"). The double alliteration ("wonder
where . . . wonder where") helps shape the folk idiom into continued existence ("be"). Whatever the metaphor of dress or form,
dignity and folk heroism transcend the merely "literary," for they
provide a design of pan-African and human struggle within the
evolution of modern consciousness. "Be."

The Panther and the Lash (1967) illustrates the decline of Langston Hughes' political imagination. Just as it had subordinated
itself to leftist clichés in 1938, so it gives way in 1967 to polemical
narratives in verse about the riots in Birmingham and Selma.
Instead of the moral voice and brilliant ironic distance of Ask
Your Mama, the importance of physical survival comes to dominate again. Where Ask Your Mama justified faith in language,
the Black idiom of irony as well as that of celebration, Panther
illustrates a final doubt about the redemptive power of literature.[21]

"Crowns and Garlands" (PL, 6) shows the limits of racial
progress sarcastically. Even artistic fame would pass:

> Put their laurels on your brow
>   Today—
> Then before you can walk
> To the neighborhood corner,

Watch them droop, wilt, fade
  Away.
Though worn in glory on my head,
They do not last a day—

While personal honors do represent substitute gratifications for the poetic figures of Christ and Cain, they assure neither lasting renown nor food for the masses.

When personal satisfaction disappears, penetrative brutality emerges naturally. The Black Panthers, a militant group during the 1960s, face the "hobnailed boot." Where religion and sex fail as substitute gratifications for the Dream, civilization deteriorates into violence or barbarism. The blame rests squarely upon those individuals in power. What is released into the society returns to haunt all who inhabit it, and those who reduce the world to the level of brutal survival endanger their own lives indirectly. What could be a moral force fails to check colonialism in the world. What began as the quest for human community as well as social freedom ("Mother to Son," 1922) has vitiated into the speaker's broken fists and ankles:

Too many years
Climbin' that hill,
'Bout out of breath.
I got my fill.

I'm gonna plant my feet
On solid ground.
If you want to see me,
Come down.   ["Down Where I Am," PL, 50]

Even more introspective, "Where? When? Which?" (PL, 97) is a neglected masterpiece. The narrator centers the concern for social and moral responsibility within a dispersed portrait of the Ku Klux Klan. The condensed power derives from brilliant similes as well as the ambiguous imagery of the seasons and horror dramatized once more within the stream of consciousness:

And the wind blows
Sharp as integration
With an edge like apartheid,
And it is winter.

The narrator transforms the night ride into psychological process,
as here warm words oppose the cold world. Linear progress reverses itself historically: "With old [and new] and not too gentle
apartheid," "Sharp as integration . . . and it is winter."

The political situation translates itself into universal type and
psychological image. The Klan that gallops in the United States
is spiritually akin to those who are responsible for brutal deaths
in South Africa.[22] The icons suggest Yeats's horseman and
Synge's *Riders to the Sea*, which Hughes certainly didn't have in
mind, though the mark of death seems equally upon his world.
When the terrorists make way on bitless horses, something worse
than pride has tethered them. What the speaker has achieved
in complexity, he deepens even further in mythic import.
Through the political context he extends the scope of meaning
to a question worthy of Socrates. When the white backlash
(1967), the "cold" repression, returns (inevitably, for it recurs
within the spiraled repetition of history), who will reclaim the
human conscience?

Which areaway, or bar,
Or station waiting room
Will not say,
Horse and horseman, outside!

For Langston Hughes, at the close of his life, the transforming
power of imagination was indeed questionable.

SEND FOR THE PIED PIPER AND LET HIM PIPE THE RATS AWAY.
SEND FOR ROBIN HOOD TO CLINCH THE ANTI-POVERTY CAM-
PAIGN.
SEND FOR THE FAIRY QUEEN WITH A WAVE OF THE WAND
TO MAKE US ALL INTO PRINCES AND PRINCESSES.
SEND FOR KING ARTHUR TO BRING THE HOLY GRAIL.

SEND FOR THE OLD MAN MOSES TO LAY DOWN THE LAW.
SEND FOR JESUS TO PREACH THE SERMON ON THE MOUNT.
["Final Call," *PL*, 30]

In recalling mythical figures from the second century B.C. to 1940, the poem gives the most attention to the period since 1958. While one group listed belongs to fantasy and the children's story, another includes national as well as racial myths. Though both the meaning and the dramatic situation are undeveloped, all the references suggest the need to impose mythic order on human chaos.

"Frederick Douglass: 1817-1895" (*PL*, 31) presents a great orator and abolitionist who performs the heroic word or action. Whether as political speech or as jeremiad, the literary text suggests the same quest for freedom. The text before us, and the one spoken as well as written in history, read the same.

> *Hear my voice!* . . .
> *Oh, to be a beast, a bird,*
> *Anything but a slave! he said.*
>
> *Who would be free*
> *Themselves must strike*
> *The first blow, he said.*

Whoever (like Robert Stepto)[23] would proclaim that literacy was his greatest priority would reduce the mythic power of the work and the man significantly. While Douglass wrote well, he also spoke well and worked for the abolition of slavery. What made him great was the completeness of his language in all spheres, for his achievement transcended any one of them. So words and actions, alike in the deep significance, well complement each other. When language becomes infused with the passionate self as well as the spiritual heroism derived from history, it can at least in part change the world. Douglass, who anthropomorphized language, enacted the determined quest for freedom as a passionate performance in dynamic will. Neither Marxism nor liberalism could explain his mythic and his cultural power, for his force came from neither myth nor ideology alone. It was *humanized and metaphoric ideology* that assured him a lasting place in Black American literary history.

Language fails not in the lack of material substance (Marx's error—or Stepto's equally) but in the loss of the imaginative commitment to make itself visionary and dynamic. Langston Hughes lived to retrace the cycle that led him time and again away from as well as toward historical tragedy. His path led once more to comic affirmation, to the apocalyptic assurance of Black and human hope. The last quality, the light so brilliantly incarnated by Black women, would reappear eventually in his fiction as Ma Rainey. Even the political world could never completely bind Hughes' literary imagination.

5

"I HEARD MA RAINEY"
The Tragicomic Imagination

The three-act tragedy *Troubled Island* (1936)[1] implies a theory for
the literary imagination of Langston Hughes. Over the years the
writer had developed an interest in Haiti, the country for which
his great-uncle had once been the American minister, and he
himself had come to read a tragic pattern in the lives of the
heroes there. Though Toussaint L'Ouverture, Dessalines, and
Christophe had each projected great dreams for the nation, including some visions for freedom and for a homeland all their
own, each faced an unfortunate end. Toussaint, tricked into
boarding a French battleship, was taken by Napoleon to prison
in Europe. Dessalines was ambushed and shot; Christophe killed
himself.[2] Yet out of their dreams and courage, during more than
a century past, the contemporary republic of Haiti emerged.

In *Troubled Island* the heroism of Dessalines in war serves him
less well in peace. Though he wants strength and greatness for
Haiti in a hurry, his people are tired, so his secretaries and gen-
erals betray him. Even his second wife, for whom he abandoned
the spouse of his slave days, contributes to the conspiracy while
she dreams of Paris. Dessalines, shot from behind by his general,
lies dead for the slave wife to recognize by the scars on his back.
As she kneels above the man she loves "in spite of all," bending

down to kiss the scars, she realizes that "his name belongs to history, but his love had been her own."

Langston Hughes had a reliable grasp of tragic conventions: the forced encounter with changed circumstance wrought inexplicably by the gods or by time; the noble quest for others turned horribly sour through the benevolent but ambitious self; the failure of poetic justice for the self from loved ones and friends; the self's own ambitious and blind betrayal, ironically on its own part, of the one who loved it truly; and, consequently, the deep shriek of the lover who mourns the dead sincerely.

If the proposition seems strained for the creator of Jesse B. Semple, the veneer of humor in Hughes' work has deceived the reader again and again, for comedy almost invariably coexists with the deeper pathos that threatens and ennobles it. Tragicomedy unifies the literary art of Hughes' entire *oeuvre*. Tragedy and comedy mark the formal range of his literary creativity as well as his perception of human life. They subsume between them the metaphors and myths of the creative world and give continuity to perhaps all his genres and subjects, including autobiography, women, and politics. Hughes understood intuitively that tragedy never excludes comedy completely, any more than the reverse is true; on the contrary, each defines its existence through the only apparent absence of the other. The comic tales of Simple (1943-65) had subsisted potentially in *The Ways of White Folks* (1934), though the comic hero himself did not appear in Hughes' work until nearly a decade later.

Langston Hughes had received the tradition of tragedy that not only presumes certain conventions in dramatic form but assumes specific metaphors and myths about the world as well. Tragedy takes into account a suspension from secular life and the actions that might find solution through innovative reason. Today we can understand what may have brought the form to an end: the decline of the organic view of the world and the related reference to mythology and symbolism. But to Langston Hughes, tragedy configured itself in ascent and descent: "[the] lament over the fall of man and the rejoicing of the resurrection of his spirit."[3]

While many of the devices Hughes inherited from classical antiquity provided comic relief instead, they functioned more profoundly as the catharsis for a suffering community: "The comic hero", says Maurice Charney, "may serve as the ritual clown of his society, acting as a scapegoat for its taboos."[4] Tales from the Native American tribes in the Southwest record the appointment annually of the clown, who provides a convenient safety valve for the repressions and neurotic tendencies of the society. In the extreme version, one that certainly exceeds the moderate taste of Langston Hughes, the clown assumes all the taboos of the community and flouts everything decent as well as sacred. In making advances to virgins and married women, he speaks forbidden words, thereby blaspheming openly against the Deity or deities. Because his actions demand divine condemnation, the auditors respond with disgust, trepidation, and terror. But the jester, or sacred fool, can violate all taboos during his time on the literal and figurative stage. Through him the audience releases itself vicariously from its most sacred customs. Such rites assure the survival and perpetuity of culture, but by limiting both individual and communal freedom, they necessarily call into tension the complex paradox of the self in conflict with society. As the social mirror to life, comedy can expose the vacuity of middle-class values; indeed, in satirizing them, it mocks the shoddy materialism pervading the United States.

In the power of his dramatic irony, Langston Hughes draws upon classical conventions to deepen the political and social awareness in his fictional world. Intuitively, he recognizes the force in the ironic pretense to stupidity and the function of the *eiron*.

Socrates is the great *eiron* of antiquity. He plays the fool, feigns ignorance, asks seemingly innocent and childlike questions that are meant to trap you. Socratic irony is still usually defined as a pretended stupidity, a disingenuousness and false naiveté, intended to mislead its hearers to produce a result strikingly different from what they counted on. . . . The *eiron* may be an entertainer and even a wise guy in some of his aspects, but Socrates was also a *sacred fool* [my emphasis], dedicated to the truth at the risk of his own life. He is our first great comic martyr. Irony is more a moral than a metaphysical assumption in comedy, and it may account for the unusual alertness demanded of the comic hero. He must, at all costs, be ready for whatever turns up, and not only ready, but also skillful, versatile, ingenious, spontaneous, and improvisatory. . . . Irony lies at the heart of comic technique. All comedy is the manipulation of deceptive appearances.[5]

In the use of foils, comedy relies less upon representative types than upon extremes and caricatures.

In the classic example, if we see someone trip on a banana peel we laugh, especially if it is a well-dressed and important person. But if we become aware that the person has broken his arm (or is otherwise seriously injured) we stop laughing. The wound draws our human pity and neutralizes laughter. In the dynamics of sick humor, however, we laugh when we see the person slip, but laugh even harder when we learn that he has broken his arm. We refuse our sympathy and insist on the full measure of retribution for persons who deserve (and need) our corrective laughter. But even sick humor would draw the line at persons whom we know and love. It is impossible to laugh at the injury of those near and dear to us, except in a condition of uncontrolled hysteria. It is this line of feeling that completely separates tragedy and comedy.[6]

What Langston Hughes acquired in spirit and tone enabled him to shape the classic conventions of tragicomedy to his own design. With the satirist he achieved self-delight in the recognition that those who spoke from within social tradition and the mainstream were often moral misfits when measured by the highest and most eternal laws, those very rules that comedy calls continuously into question. Still unwilling to console himself in sick humor, Hughes almost never demanded the full penalty of retribution; he was willing to forget and forgive, though both processes became more difficult for him at life's end. While his comic impulse and natural congeniality directed him toward polite integration into American society, the tragic history of slavery in the United States and his destiny to oppose its legacy through the written word kept him isolated. His role went through and beyond that of the Black American to that of the free thinker and the moral individual in society. Ever the comedian, he designed small resolutions in marriage for his plots, yet ever the tragedian, he recognized that freedom transcended laughter. So comedy signified yet almost never contained his Dream.

In "Berry" (1934), one of his earliest and most tragic tales about racial discrimination during the first half of the century, Hughes recreates not classic tragedy but rather Judaeo-Christian tragedy rooted in the sociohistory of Black America during the mid-1930s.[7] When a Scandinavian kitchen boy quits without notice, Mrs. Osborn, supervisor of Dr. Renfield's home of crippled children, wires to Jersey City for a replacement. Encountering Black Milberry Jones subsequently, she is surprised by the race of the prospective employee and wonders immediately about an appropriate place for him to sleep. After taking up the problem with Dr. Renfield, her superior, she hires the youngster (his age is not given) but agrees to pay him only eight dollars instead of the ten that the white boy had received. Despite his industrious work, Berry loses his job when a child falls from a wheelchair through little or no fault on Berry's part. But the story of racial injustice moves toward neither a comic resolution in which all is well nor a truly tragic one. Rather, the plot unifies a complex of symbolic movements suggesting the fall of Berry, whose tragic flaw is Christian love. But he does have the restorative power of storytelling: "Then when the time came to go in for rest before dinner, Milberry helped push the wheel chairs, a task which the nurses hated. And he held the hands of those kids with braces and twisted limbs as they hobbled along. He told them stories, and he made up jokes in the sun on the beach. And one rainy afternoon on the porch he sang songs, old southern Negro songs, funny ones that the children loved (WF 178).

Renfield and Osborn, who have "eyes" for each other, never "see" the humanity in Berry at all. The metaphor of the invisible Black, a figurative type in the fiction of Richard Wright and Ralph Ellison, complements an equally powerful emblem: the children are crippled. The first situation implies the cruelty that people impose upon each other; the second suggests the fate that God or the gods may have determined for them.

Whatever the claims of "Berry" for the status of tragedy, the messianic overtones imply comedy. Berry himself, in his illuminative stories, resembles the sun shining through the driving rain. His expressive form is soul, the symbolic source for Black music, literature, and art. While the innocent children image themselves through the sun, the more experienced and corrupted adults show all the bleakness of the literal rain outside. Though the narrator in The Ways of White Folks dedicates the collection of short fiction to Noel Sullivan—Hughes' patron in Carmel, California, in 1934—the signature reads "Berry." It is emblematic that he pushes "a couple of wheel chairs at a time to the sand's edge." Here the children seem to inhabit a world of divine comedy, and here the harmony of good and evil appears almost able to resolve itself in the end. But the elders perform their learned rites of exorcism in the world of tragic time. They need acceptance and money; they seek the "prizes" of secular comedy.

While the presence of Judaeo-Christian redemption in "Berry" alters potential tragedy into comedy, "Father and Son" (1934)— possibly Langston Hughes' best-crafted fiction—more closely follows the conventions of tragedy. The story is about Bert, the mulatto son of Cora, a Black woman, and about Colonel Thomas Norwood, a white plantation owner in Georgia. Forty-eight pages in length (nearly four times as long as any other entry in White Folks), it reflects a subject that had long been a preoccupation for Hughes. "Mulatto," a poem published in the Saturday Review *of Literature* (27 Jan. 1927), had shown a youth uncertain of his own racial identity, and a three-act tragedy with the same title was produced at the Vanderbilt Theater on Broadway in 1935; it was Hughes' first full-length play and professionally produced drama. *Mulatto*, in turn, became the basis for the libretto of *The Barrier*, an opera produced by the Columbia University Opera Workshop on 18 January 1950.

The plot of the prose story "Father and Son" has a dramatic structure. First comes the inciting incident of Bert's arrival back home in Georgia. Then the path leads, through Bert's climactic conflict with a white female clerk, to his inevitable confrontation with his father. After he murders Norwood, Bert is pursued by a lynch mob, as might be expected for the time. And just as Bert's advance toward a final reckoning contributes to the dramatic action, his having been beaten by Norwood during his childhood—an event that recurs through the multiple consciousness of Bert, Norwood, and Cora—completes the symbolic animalism at work in the story.

Such narrative codes determine the mood and impact, yet exist outside of the dramatic action. "Colonel Thomas Norwood stood in his doorway at the Big House looking down the dusty plantation road. Today his youngest son was coming home. A heavy Georgia spring filled the morning air with sunshine and earth-perfumes. It made the old man feel strangely young again. Bert was coming home" (*WF*, 200). Antonymous images of night and day set the tragic tone as well as imply the dynamic passage of time. And Bert, the mirror-image of Norwood himself years before, must turn inevitably from facing his father back to the world of tragic time.

The narrator of the story makes clear the disintegration of the communal and holy bond. But the symbolic oppositions between Norwood and Bert run more deeply. Taken together, the two men share a responsibility that to Hughes can "never be washed away." To him the metaphors of uncleanliness—responses that are intense, moral, and personal as well as mythic—go back to the Scottsboro boys, falsely accused in 1931 of raping two white prostitutes. Then the scene was a freight train steaming from Chattanooga to Memphis, but now the apocalyptic counterpoint to southern racism appears through lyrical streams of consciousness.[8] "In the chemistry lab at school, did you ever hold a test tube, pouring in liquids and powders and seeing nothing happen until a *certain* liquid or a *certain* powder is poured in and then everything begins to smoke and fume, bubble and boil, hiss to foam, and sometimes even explode? The tube is suddenly full of action and movement and life. Well, there are people like those certain liquids or powders; at a given moment . . . "(WF, 220). The movement is tragic because the solemn tone subverts harmony and pleasure in order to reveal the malevolent force in nature. What else but tragedy, given the profound isolation and alienation of the individual from his or her community, suits a family which, like the Norwoods, can never sit down at once to dinner? It is a group for which Cora shells peas in the big house at the very beginning, and even then the tall windows face westward toward death.

As in classic tragedy, death is foreshadowed in the destiny of Bert Norwood. Though it apparently purges troublemakers like him from the social world, and so allows nature to resume harmony temporarily, its rituals violate all laws of human decency in this instance. In viewing Bert's arrival with "bucked eyes," his brother Willie knows early on that trouble is coming. Cora goes to warn Bert about the severe consequences of resisting the Colonel's philosophy: "I didn't bear you for no white man to kill" (WF, 230). Higgins, the county politician and postmaster, cautions Norwood on the phone: "There ain't been no race trouble in our country for three years—since the Deekins lynching but I'm telling you . . . folks ain't gonna stand for this. I'm speaking on the quiet; but I see ahead. What happened this morning in the post office ain't none too good" (WF, 228). When cotton prices had dropped earlier during the torrid summer, white sharecroppers became restless; then Talbot and the storekeeper beat to death a fieldhand who "talked high" to a white planter. Even the revival Norwood orders when shots about town disturb Black laborers fails miserably. Neither melodramatic diversions nor lyrical friezes redeem "Father and Son" from the overwhelming conventions of tragedy.

While several actions in the subplots are too sentimental and awkward, they do help to reveal the connection between the psychology of power and the relationship of one culture's rise and another's fall. Both Bert and Norwood function within the same myth so much that the plantation appears first as a big rise on the horizon but seems quite fallen in the end—not the physical structure but the premise upon which it stands: "The Colonel sensed it in his out-stretched hand and his tall young body—and had turned his back and walked into the house. Cora with her hands in the cool water where the plums were, suddenly knew in her innermost soul a period of time had closed for her" (WF, 221).

Many of the stock devices are predictable. Higgins, who believes that Bert does not know "his place," provokes the Colonel, who decries that "yellow buck." What particularly angers Norwood in his implicit obligation to Bert as his son as well as Bert's obvious insistence that the Colonel live up to responsibilities. To this end, the verbs are lofty indeed. The Colonel "damns" the son and "raves" while Cora "weeps." Often the action takes place in the past perfect tense ("night had come") when the past impinges on the present. Yet even the melodramatic tendency does not undermine the tragic effect in "Father and Son," because the narrator invokes lyrical friezes regarding Bert: "There are people (you've probably noted it also) who have the unconscious faculty of making the world spin around themselves, throb and expand, contract and go dizzy. Then, when they are gone away, you feel sick and lonesome and meaningless" (WF, 220). Though the form is short prose, the mythic undercurrent is elegiac.

But elegiac form exists only to reverse the movement from life to death back finally from death to life. Without either praise or celebration, tragedy ennobles the self to face fatality. Elegy, on the contrary, celebrates the dead figure who achieves a moral ascent over the would-be tragic end. Here is one of the most brilliant acrostics Langston Hughes ever wrote:

> "Lawd, chile, Bert's come home . . . "
> "Lawd, chile, and he said . . . "
> "Lawd, chile, he said . . . "
> "Lawd, chile . . . "
> "Lawd . . . "

Read from top left corner to the bottom right, the verbal graphic ends in despair, "Lawd . . . " The expression from the left corner at the bottom, straight on up to the top, reveals an equal despair for the acknowledged God from whom no explanation will come: "Lawd / Lawd." In the descent from the top to the bottom of the second column, an equally tragic wail sounds through human generations, "chile / chile." And like the fall implied there, the folk regression in the third tab to the right ends in tragic noth- ingness: "Bert's /and / he said / . . . " Only the graphic pattern from the far right corner to the bottom left and back to the top right promises Judaeo-Christian redemption: "Come home / he said / he said /Lawd, chile / Lawd"; "/Lawd / Lawd, chile / he said / and he said / come home . . . "9

Where such placements alone do not suffice to sustain the tragic mood, especially at the end of the misfortune, the narrator draws skillfully upon the thematic devices of death, insanity, and metaphysical chaos. He exploits as well the conventions of the cosmic soliloquy and the wail. After Bert shoots himself—thereby depriving the mob of the presumed delight of lynching him— Talbot bursts in as Cora is pulling feverishly at the body of the dead Colonel. When he asks a friend to arrange for a posse, she is aware that "night had come." In a subsequent soliloquy she bids the dead colonel rise, reminding him of all the occasions for which she served him well in bed and demanding recompense now in the form of her son's life. From far off in the distance, she hears the hounds pursuing Bert, while the body at her feet remains unmoving. Finally, she goes upstairs, leaving the Colonel's corpse lying on the floor. As the hounds continue to bay, she prepares a hiding place in the attic for Bert, who has already shot himself but whom she fantasizes about as still coming home to die. Her statement "night had come" extends to the metaphysical universe.

By insisting that the Colonel still rides outside with the mob, Cora upsets the undertaker, yet her statement rings true for those who have read great tragedy. What preoccupies the speaker is the dynamic movement of evil.[10] However incongruent it seems that Norwood, the father of several Blacks, would participate in lynch mobs, it follows naturally the illogic in southern race relations historically. And Cora's wail situates her within a vital tradition as well.

There comes a moment in Mutter Courage when the soldiers carry in the dead body of Schweizerkas. They suspect that he is the son of Courage but are not quite certain. She must be forced to identify him. I saw Helen Weigel act the scene with the East Berlin ensemble, though acting is a paltry word for the marvel of her incarnation. As the body of her son was laid before her, she merely shook her head in moot denial. The soldiers compelled her to look again. Again she gave no sign of recognition, only a dead stare. As the body was carried off, Weigel looked the other way and tore her mouth wide open. The shape of the gesture was that of the screaming horse in Picasso's Guernica. The sound that came out was raw and terrible beyond any description I could give of it. But in fact there was no sound. Nothing. The Sound was total silence. It was silence which screamed and screamed through the whole theater so that the audience lowered its head as before a gust of wind. And that scream inside the silence seemed to be the same as Cassandra's when she divines the reek of blood in the house of Atreus. It was the same wild cry with which the tragic imagination first marked our sense of life. The same wild and pure lament over man's inhumanity and waste of man.[11]

Hughes balanced such tragic imagination with prose of another kind. In "Big Round World" (1957), one of the most skillful and representative of the comic tales, Simple tells a folk story to the middle-class interlocutor: "The other day a white man asked where is my home. . . . I said, 'What do you mean, where is my home—as big and round as the world is? Do you mean where I live now? Or where I *did* live? Or where I was born?' "[12] Simple is mocking the imprecision of the inquiry. While the wordplay is innocent, it implies a profound understanding of cultural difference.

The white assumes a linear movement through Western time from the past through the present to the future. He assumes an advance into tragic death. But Simple draws upon the African roots in which past, present, and future occupy different levels of hierarchical existence within one continuous time. While the white believes the racial self has been fragmented over time, Simple thinks the self has been divided only across varying levels of space. Though Simple's view of life assumes the existence of a consciousness that informs space and time, the white man's posture focuses more particularly on a place within history. When the white clarifies his intention to know the state of Simple's origin in the United States, Simple insists that the two of them were born in the same place. And though Simple fancies himself generally a race man, he goes on to deny that he himself looks like any "Mau Mau."

Having been the racial chauvinist on the one hand, Simple has leaped wildly to embrace universality on the other. As he shifts dexterously and unabashedly from one state to the other, his position undergoes an almost magical transformation. To him, the wild leaps of contradiction and inconsistency pose no incongruity at all, at least none less ridiculous than those that take place in a society supposedly based on reason and morality yet still allowing racial segregation in the 1950s. When the white refers to "our language," the joke is on both men: the ancestor of the one had spoken German, that of the other surely some

African tongue. So language is less a sign of ancestry than of the community that shapes and adapts it to use. The joke turns finally upon Boyd, the middle-class listener. "Exiles and escapees from the high and middle classes . . . are usually only on detached service with the low people. They are slumming, as it were, temporarily resting from their high responsibilities or postponing the moment when they will be forced to take up their options. Youths on holiday and on the make are evident in this category, pleasantly floating on the island of past adolescent indulgence. The resolution of the comic action usually brings this idyllic period to an end."[13] When the interlocutor says he was born not west of Georgia, as Simple has understood him to mean, but west of the Mississippi, he resists the southern stereotype (but one grounded in historical fact) as well. Comedy still represents itself as cyclic return. Says Simple: "I have not traveled much, but I have been a few places. And one thing I do know is that if you go around the world, in the end you get right back to where you started from—which is really going around in circles. I wish the world was flat so a man could travel straight on forever to different places and not come back to the same place." He wishes that the comic relief, the very form of his fictional existence, were real and that its happy ending would confirm an eternal future of harmony. "In that case," the interlocutor responds, "it [the world] would have to stretch to infinity . . . since nothing is endless except eternity. There the spirit lives and grows forever."

As "Big Round World" sustains its comic appeal through such wild flights of fantasy on Simple's part, and through some delusions of grandeur, the narrative imagination provides a really noble tone. It is impossible to dismiss Simple's dream of being a Black giant who, like Joe Louis, wants to end racial prejudice. Eventually, he would raise himself to the edge of the cosmic world to which the physical laws of Galileo no longer apply. Simple would shake England until it abandons colonialism and helps to end apartheid in South Africa. When he daydreams

about transforming Australia into a "colored" continent, the interlocutor says rightly, "You have an imagination *par excellence* . . . which is French for great." Simple, carried away now
by his own rhetoric, imagines a sneeze that would literally blow
the Ku Klux Klan away; he dismisses Jim Crow from the South
with a mere clap of the hands. In bringing the segregation in
musical theater to an end, he would shake racists from his shoes
like ants. Where battles were raging throughout the world, he
would implement peace, and he would have exposed in the process the discrepancy between Christian word and deed.

Even his blues fantasy proves insufficient to resolve issues so
profound, and so does the Judaeo-Christian rhetoric of apocalyptic redemption. To propose that one hilarious storyteller who
drinks beer in a Harlem bar, or any individual for that matter,
could defeat social atrocities more than four hundred years old
is to be absurd. But Hughes thrived on placing Simple in unexpected contexts anyway.

> The fool in Shakespeare functions against a background of
> real fools, who were part of noble households in the Eliza-
> bethan period, either natural fools crazed in the wits or
> professional jesters, or some combinations of the
> two. . . . The fool understands Lear's folly as no one else
> can, and he speaks by allowance and permission. In a sense
> he is totally fearless, despite Lear's continual references to
> the whip, by which the fool becomes the *ritual scapegoat*
> [my emphasis] for everything that is troubling the old man,
> but he is . . . a philosophic and moral instructor as well.
> Since he is completely outside the social hierarchy, he is
> free to speak and to act without constraint; it is as if, except
> for his role as ritual clown, he had no separate being at all.
> He exists for the sake of King Lear: to mitigate his passion
> and to offer him an elemental commiseration and comfort,
> and also, in another sense, be the son Lear never had.[14]

And Simple shares the privilege.

"Shadow of the Blues" (1953), a bar tale about the tragicomic

imagination, resolves the issues of history and death somewhat
more humorously.[15] With dramatic immediacy the scene begins
in medias res: Simple has more than a hundred dollars in his
possession, for he has not paid the rent or gone to the laundry
to redeem his clean clothes. He has saved the money to pay for
a divorce from his wife so that he can marry Joyce, his girlfriend,
meanwhile relying on his good friend Boyd, the interlocutor, for
drinks in the Harlem bar. He has, he says, "sacrificed" for the
expected good day, and Boyd wisecracks, "So have I." When a
quarter drops into the jukebox, the two agree that no singer there
ranks with Bessie Smith of old. Subsequently, the plot turns on
the debate as to who is older than whom. Each man invokes
archival references, especially tributes to the great blues singers,
any detailed knowledge of whom would date the other's lifetime.
When the interlocutor brings up the Smith sisters, the famous
blues singers, Simple laughs: "Boy, you must be older than me
because I only heard tell of Mamie. I'm glad I am not as ageable
as you. You's an *old* Negro." The tone goes from the hilarious
to the serious as the structure passes from comedy to tragicomedy.
At first the random subjects seem light—toys, drama, women,
growing up, the jazz age—yet the tone reverses itself when Simple
remembers the days before the advent of refrigerators. Still for
each of the interlocutor's jibes, Simple has an immediate retort,
and the comic digressions into signs of historical time—butter
hung in a well to keep cool, pennies worth nickels and the
certainty of inflation, the purchase of an Elgin watch at the price
of a dollar for a friend's birthday—conceal the covert shift in
the tone and structure. Then their memories turn to Madam
Walker, whose innovation in hair straightening for Black women
would allow her daughter A'Lelia to give great parties one day
during the Harlem Renaissance.

When the interlocutor concludes this comic suspension in-
tentionally, he appears to have emerged victorious in the delightful play on the dozens, the verbal challenge of making one's
listener the butt of the joke. Almost indifferently he makes his
best move: "Let me ask you about one more personality we

forgot—Ma Rainey." In a nearly religious shout, Simple acknowledges her greatness and refuses to curb his enthusiasm even
when the interlocutor points to such an admission as the decisive
sign of Simple's age: "You're ancient, man, you're ancient." But
neither convenient malapropisms nor the prospect of defeat can
blunt seriousness now:

> Ma Rainey were too dark to be a mist [myth]. But she really
> could sing the blues. I will not deny Ma Rainey, even to
> hide my age. Yes I heard her! I am proud of hearing her.
> To tell the truth, if I stop and listen, I can still hear her:
>
> > Wonder where my . . .
> > Easy rider's gone . . .
> > Done left me . . .
> > New gold watch in pawn . . .
> >
> > Trouble in mind, I'm blue—
> > But I won't be always.
> > The sun's gonna shine in
> > My back door someday . . .
>
> One thing I got to be thankful for, even if it do make me
> as old as you, is I heard Ma Rainey.

Here the Blues, like comedy, arrests the movement of tragic
and linear time, even the certainty of death. To Langston
Hughes, the narrator in the tragicomic world and the great blues
singers are the same: they convert tragic time into laughter and
the reaffirmation of the human spirit. Like comedy, blues confront the problems in the world and the unexplained injustice
decreed by self-appointed gods yet still signify the heroic endurance of the artistic self. While tragedy brings life to an end
(Rainey had died in 1939), comedy promises poetic justice.
Comedy strikes a parallel with Judaeo-Christian redemption: "I
got to be thankful . . . I heard Ma Rainey." "Ma" imposed the
comic metaphor upon tragic history, no matter how wry and
concealed the humor would become: "I'm blue but I won't be
always. The suns's gonna shine in my back door someday." For

the slave in the nineteenth century, as for the Black worker on plantations at the turn of this one and for some domestic servants today, Rainey promised an end to the era of rear entrances. Though her vision was apocalyptic in tone, it was comic in structure.

Hughes' own short fiction imposed the comic structure on Black American history. Where events were calamitous, he endowed them with the humorous assertion of his own indomitability. Gertrude "Ma" Rainey had begun singing the blues in 1902, the year of Langston Hughes' birth, and his life, like hers, would come full circle. Born in Columbus, Georgia, in 1886, by the age of fifteen she had married Will Rainey and begun performances with his troupe, the Rabbit Foot Minstrels. At various times such musicians as Louis Armstrong, Buster Bailey, Charles Green, and Fletcher Henderson were all among her acquaintances. Though she retired in 1933, the year before *The Ways of White Folks* was published, Hughes would simply transform the tragic tone of her life.

The reference to Bessie Smith is even more incongruous, though ironically appropriate for comic purposes. Born into poverty in Chattanooga, Tennessee, she was discovered at the age of thirteen by Ma Rainey. After touring with the Rabbit Foot Minstrels, Smith gradually achieved recognition in Black vaudeville. In 1923, three years before the publication of Hughes' first book, she had made her first recording, "Down Hearted Blues." During the Great Depression her career declined because record sales were down, and she had personal problems. In 1937 she died in Mississippi following an automobile accident—because the nearest hospital was for whites only, and she was refused admission. Recognized today among the greatest talents in jazz, Bessie was one of the most gifted blues singers. What the comic writer laughs at in "Shadow of the Blues" is not the tragedy of her own Black American history—for in this regard he is too close and too deeply moved—but those who will never understand the resolve and the quality of her heroism.

"Lynn Clarisse," one of the last Simple tales (1965), uses

Simple's middle-class cousin from the South to stress responsibility in Simple's present life and, perhaps, in Boyd's future.[16] When the interlocutor asks the protagonist—a debutante, reader, and graduate of Fisk University—why she has a cousin like Simple, she has no need to invoke middle-class apologies: "He is in the family and is one relative who happens to be down with it. . . . I love the cat, and I love his Harlem." Freed now to express his own emotions, for the power of comedy derives from masking and unmasking, the auditor confirms, "I do, too."

But Simple has described Clarisse as a "girl" whose mind does not transcend the classroom and whose thought is conventional. In face, the charges better fit the interlocutor—and what has Simple himself done except sit at the bar and talk? Clarisse, whatever her background in the "Black Ivy League" or her readings in Sartre and Genet, has been on the front line for civil rights: she has participated in freedom rides; her neck bears the scar of a southern police beating; and once her shoulder was broken as well. To sustain humor in the face of such disfiguration would violate the moral sense. Yet the interlocutor tries valiantly to suspend social history and tragic time. When he asks Lynn Clarisse if she's really "colored," she quips, "Are you blind?" The speaker has questioned her racial awareness; she counters effectively with laughter. Clarisse, so dark in hue, shows Boyd that he can achieve status without the denial of racial pride. To her, the trip north is merely a tidy diversion from the tragic time to be reentered soon; she has come to New York in part to acquire new books, and Simple has brought her to the cafe.

The narrative recalls the "clean well-lighted place" on New Year's Eve in Paris where, as 1937 turned to 1938, Hughes and Seki Sano had renewed their friendship just before the advent of World War II. Then, as in "Lynn Clarisse," Hughes' tone suggested the uncertainty of human destiny, and he shaped his tone for 1965 through the imagery he had used to portray war then. In "Lynn Clarisse" the narrator can conceal the bond between the inner world (comic) and the metaphysically outer world (tragic) only for a while. During her stay in New York,

Clarisse means to complete a cultural itinerary that includes attendance at productions or performances by Sammy Davis, Jr., Ruby Dee, Gilbert Prince, Diana Sands, and LeRoi Jones (Amiri Baraka)—"I've got to keep up with my own culture"—because such plays would not be produced in the South. The closure becomes tragicomic, for haste and the need to be responsible extend to the epic dimension: "And me, I have got something to do right now, interrupted Simple at the edge of our booth. I have got to go home." The high style is used for seriousness rather than for rhetorical play or bombast. Closure appears not as a trick that the imagination can dodge but as the imminent return of cosmic chaos and tragic time.

Because the comic tale has already interrupted tragic time, Simple's own remark interrupts an interruption; it returns the auditor to the sociohistorical world. Even though the restoration brings him to the metaphoric edge, to the literal brink of the booth from which he speaks and to a point from which imagination nearly dominates the external world, responsibility intervenes: "I have got to go home." As Simple motions his way to the door, Boyd remarks that all married men should be home at midnight. When Simple turns the tables on him shrewdly by suggesting that so should all "young ladies," such as Lynn Clarisse, Boyd remains in the bar. Before his departure, however, Simple drops a quarter into the jukebox so that Boyd can listen to Nina Simone sing. What closes the scene marks perhaps the second most brilliant acrostic in the literary world of Langston Hughes:

> "Good night, old boy." [Simple]
> "Good night, my ertswhile friend." [Boyd]
> "Good night, Mr. Boyd." [Lynn Clarisse]
> "Good night."
>   [All, including the narrator and Langston Hughes]

Where the high style provokes no laughter, it carries the deep tone of serious loss and dynamic time. Read downward to the

left margin, the closure sounds, "Good night / Good night," and
then in the descent from the top left corner to the bottom right,
"Good night / my ertswhile friend / Mr. Boyd." And, from bottom left to top right, the design concludes, "Good night / Mr.
Boyd / my ertswhile friend / old boy."

Why would the comic world of Langston Hughes turn suddenly
upon the diction of *Hamlet*, *Faustus*, or even *The Waste Land*?
To revel in the triviality of human problems, to delight in incongruity as well as irony, means to divert the serious view of
social tragedy. Diversion fosters irresponsibility. Because the process minimizes the need to support change, even the humorous
writer shares complicity with the order he condemns: "There is
no way for the structure of comedy to avoid the prevailing mores,
and the end of comedy, which is a much more conservative genre
than tragedy, must reflect the ends of society. No pun is intended
on 'end' and 'ending,' although it is obvious that the endings of
comedy enforce orthodoxy.[17]

When Langston Hughes died on 22 May 1967, Toy Harper,
his friend for many years, was in the intensive care unit at the
same Polyclinic Hospital in New York City. Often Langston and
Toy's husband, Emerson, had said that she had "supernatural
powers," and on this occasion she told the nurse about a dis-
turbing dream: "Langston Hughes had climbed atop a pole to
reach toward a tower and had fallen."[18] Because the metaphor
brilliantly signifies Hughes' tragic imagination, it inspires a reconsideration of his work and life.

Langston Hughes may well have read the pattern of rise and
fall in the biography of Dessalines because the tragic encounter
with social history highlights the comic quest for human freedom.
While social history is sad, the human spirit is hopeful. The
duality, the awareness of tragic evil in the world yet the insistence
on subverting tragedy while driving through to the happy end—
the blues transcendence—marks the bond between outer and inner
worlds, between presence and absence, between form and meaning.
The tragic play and the comic counterplay do indeed reveal the
literary imagination. It was all indeed so deceptively profound.

CONCLUSION

But as undisciplined and unwise as man is, no matter
how many times he may decline and fall, there always
seems to be some representative of the species left
around to rise up and try again.

—Langston Hughes, *Chicago Defender*
16 October 1948

Wonder, for Langston Hughes, meant the freeing of the speaker
from tragic time temporarily, yet it marked the conflict or tension
that gave intellectual depth as well as feeling to the aesthetic
world. Often the reader encounters the oppositions of fact and
truth when the world provokes conflict between conscience and
power. Though Hughes inherited the modern tradition of the
confessional self, which speaks through the varied forms of autobiography, lyric, and short fiction, he drew upon the ancient
idea of literary discourse as a public and communal performance.
His was a dynamic ritual that celebrated life and ancestry as song
does. In an outstanding poem such as "The Negro Speaks of
Rivers," the undramatized listener establishes a communal bond
with the speaker. Yet no single genre ever imprisoned Langston
Hughes, who rebelled against formal limits as easily as he opposed
social ones.

The organization of this book has followed the chronology by
which he introduced lyrics and other literary forms into his work.
From the roots of Black folk culture he discovered the art of
storytelling and music early on. From his own travel around the
world, especially to Paris and then on to Madrid in the 1920s
and 1930s, he extrapolated the personal metaphors of quest and
hunger. What he valued in the spirituals, he appreciated in jazz,

blues, and flamenco. Maupassant had placed nineteenth-century France at the center of portraiture; Hughes would put Harlem there instead. Though the urban environment remained his home for most of his life, he had learned about the power of symbolic scenes in nature early, during his teens.

Many of his literary friezes, his emblems of artists and art such as those involving Duse and Seki Sano, rank with the most brilliant in the literature of the United States. While many literary historians have read his texts as social documents only, able scholars such as Richard K. Barksdale and Faith Berry have helped balance the approach of structuralists, or even poststructuralists, who would divorce literature from history as well as from culture. But the theoretical debate is academic only, for structuralists usually ignore the folk expression of Langston Hughes in their haste to favor the surrealism of Ralph Ellison.

Hughes himself would probably not have frowned completely upon the choice. After all, he dedicated *Montage of A Dream Deferred* (1951) to Ellison and Ellison's wife, Fanny. But any preference between the two authors would depend neither upon purely aesthetic judgment—for any such thing is impossible—nor upon merely ideological requirements. The major difference would stem from whether one prefers a pervasively comic or tragic vision of the world or whether one looks for irony in the discrete text or in the whole. At stake is the heroic potential to make comedy release us finally from modern absurdity, including our pervasive sense of a tragic universe from which even the gods have disappeared.

Certainly both Hughes and Ellison worked diligently to transform the folk resources of the same culture. Both writers profited from the legacy of folk and comic irony that dates back to the period of 1830-50, the time of the early seculars; both projected blues performance as transcendence and defiance. Hughes did so, for example, in "Weary Blues" and "Trumpet Player"; Ellison did so in some seminal essays in *Shadow and Act*. While Ellison probably focused more on transcendence in *Invisible Man* and on comic resolution, as the two processes set the American Dream into relief, Hughes probably revealed a bit more about tragic death in "Father and Son" as well as in *Mulatto*.

But the two authors differ in degree only, for even Ellison probably never struggled more than Hughes did to find the proper balance between self and world. What distinguished Hughes was the great sweep and effort in the literary imagination. Any number of outstanding writers superseded or would supersede him in the mastery of one or more genres. Frederick Douglass did so in the slave narrative (*Life and Times*), Gwendolyn Brooks in the brilliant sequence of sonnets ("children of the poor"), James Baldwin in the contemplative essay (*No Name in the Street*), and David Bradley and Toni Morrison in the mythic novel (*Cheyneysville Incident* and *Song of Solomon*).

But the great reach and great innocence made Langston Hughes deceptively profound as well as incomparably enduring. Through the autobiographical imagination he expressed the bond between history and self as well as that between fact and interpretation. While he assigned to himself the task of recording cultural history, the pattern of the events imaged as well as the values he decoded—the myth of them—would live beyond Harlem. *The Big Sea* kept the record of the milestones in his career yet preserved the fictive self imperfectly.

Whatever the importance of autobiography to Langston Hughes, the image of the Black woman signified the rise and fall of his literary imagination. Whether because of his grandmother, who read him stories on the porch in Kansas, or his mother, who had some literary skills of her own, the commitment extended from the heroic speaker in "Mother to Son" in 1922 to the hilarious "Madam" in 1949. What made the Black woman central to Hughes' world was her role as griot and keeper of memories. Like the autobiographer, she sought to keep alive the rites that facilitated the passage from slavery to freedom. Hers was often the lyrical imagination. It was not the private and esoteric implosion that modernism would favor but a rite of celebration shared with the audience.

While the chorus implied there was almost always invisible

for Hughes, it had a power even in silence; it confirmed a musical transcendence, whether through the anonymous piano player in "Weary Blues," the unnamed trumpet player in the poem so titled, or the singer such as Billie Holiday. Usually, dynamic art triumphed over suffering and death. The lyrical imagination, like the comic kind, froze tragic time.

But such linear time is in part only an illusion, and so is "history," which often reshapes itself in new guises for the future. To Hughes, John Brown and Frederick Douglass were two very different kinds of abolitionists in the nineteenth century, yet both performed equally within the human melodrama of Good and Evil. Their personal signatures or forms of poetic vision and morality, like literature as well as human progress, were deceptively complex, inextricably bound.

Though the literary imagination informed the life and work of Langston Hughes, the skeptic will still have doubts about the critical method in this volume. Why should I impose a formal and even theoretical posture on a folk poet who vowed to achieve simplicity? Well, writers often display complexity and depth far greater than they intend. Only part of the creative act is conscious on the author's part, and a portion of the pleasure of criticism derives in part from the illumination of a truth or possibility that the writer has concealed from even himself.

"What if," someone will surely ask, "the symbolic representation of racial consciousness derived from slavery and Jim Crow is irrelevant to the study of high art and universality, as well as to even the most 'objective' literary history?" While some scholars may indeed evince such lack of interest, responsible criticism proposes to justify the grounds of praise, whatever they may be. The reader seeks to establish some objective proof for what began as a subjective response. While the readings here are probing and speculative, they have emerged naturally from the text.

What, for Hughes, were lyric and comedy and tragedy? What were all these "Western" forms? Doesn't Hughes belong to the great oral tradition? So he does, but no race can make a sacred claim on the forms of the human imagination. Unless literary genres have arisen from the genes of some supreme race (and the point would seem preposterous), literary typology is universal. If myth or type is, so forms are as well. Why write yet another book about this author, especially if not to preempt Arnold Rampersad's definitive *Life of Langston Hughes* (1986)? Students have looked in vain for a sustained examination of the creative voices and forms in Langston Hughes' literary world, for the strategies that shape the depth and meaning in the texts. But most of all, they need to decode the patterns of his voice and the images through which he interpreted and transformed his historical world. Though Hughes had a debt to history—especially from "The Negro Speaks of Rivers" (1921) to the reprint of "Daybreak in Alabama" (1967)—and though he himself intended to leave behind a record for posterity, a metaphoric power and meaning elevated him beyond the height of even his most distinguished critics. He was not only a historical curiosity, a dedicated recorder, but a Black craftsman and myth-maker. Ever watchful for the Klan at his back, he turned now and then to *wonder* about a new southern morning.

How did the major five components of his writing and imagination work *together*? Why must Langston Hughes and his work be reconsidered? It is necessary to appreciate the way that each creative form merges finally with the others throughout the Hughes *oeuvre*. An inquiry into five genres, revealed through successive windows as dimensional frames opened individually on Harlem and the universe, develops finally into a holistic assessment of his literary imagination. The tragic and comic impulses distinguish themselves finally as the unifying quality. In *The Big Sea* and *I Wonder as I Wander* the lyric reflection on the New Year of 1938 suspended the record of impending World War II. Even before then the lyric celebration of the Black and human self ("I've Known Rivers") had already looked beyond slavery and the subsequent racial segregation in the southern United States. When political history came to the fore sometimes and dominated many poems less distinguished than "Madrid—1937" (for example, "Jim Crow's Last Stand"), the lyrical imagination waned, yet the lyric intensity appeared once more through the tragicomic balance of the short fiction. Particularly in "Shadow of the Blues," tragicomedy was the most comprehensive shape for the literary imagination. It was indeed the formal analogue to Black woman, a spiritual figure self-robed in ascendant light. Tragicomedy was the supergenre, for it subsumed and transcended nearly all the others. It was itself, indeed, a kind of wonder.

NOTES

INTRODUCTION

1. *WW*, 405.

2. See, e.g., Stephen Henderson, *Understanding the New Black Poetry: Black Speech and Black Music as Poetic References* (New York: Morrow, 1972).

3. James Engell, *The Creative Imagination* (Cambridge, Mass.: Harvard Univ. Press, 1981), vii-x. See also Albert William Levi, *Literature, Philosophy, and the Imagination* (Bloomington: Indiana Univ. Press, 1962); Jan Wilbanks, *Hume's Theory of Imagination* (The Hague: Martinus Nijoff, 1968); Lawrence Lerner, *The Literary Imagination: Essays on Literature and Society* (London: Barnes & Noble, 1982); John Spenser Hill, ed., *Imagination in Coleridge* (Totowa, N.J.: Rouman & Littlefield, 1978).

4. Hill, *Imagination in Coleridge*, 3; Wilbanks, *Hume's Theory*, 79-80.

5. Donald C. Dickinson, *A Bio-Bibliography of Langston Hughes, 1902-1967* (Hamden, Conn: Archon Books, 1967); Therman B. O'Daniel, ed., *Langston Hughes: Black Genius* (New York: Morrow, 1971), 211-41; idem, "An Updated Selected Bibliography," *Black American Literature Forum* 15 (1981): 104-7 (special issue on Langston Hughes, ed. R. Baxter Miller); R. Baxter Miller, *Langston Hughes and Gwendolyn Brooks: A Reference Guide* (Boston: G.K. Hall, 1978).

6. See James A. Emanuel, *Langston Hughes* (New York: Twayne, 1967); Onwuchekwa Jemie, *Langston Hughes: An Introduction to the*

Poetry (New York: Columbia Univ. Press, 1976); Richard K. Barksdale, *Langston Hughes: The Poet and His Critics* (Chicago: American Library Association, 1977); Faith Berry, *Langston Hughes: Before and Beyond Harlem* (Westport, Conn: Lawrence Hill, 1983); Arnold Rampersad, *The Life of Langston Hughes*, 2 vols. (New York: Oxford Univ. Press, 1986, 1988).

7. Lemuel A. Johnson, *The Devil, the Gargoyle, and the Buffoon: The Negro as Metaphor in Western Literature* (Port Washington, N.Y.: Kennikat Press, 1971); Edward J. Mullen, ed., *Langston Hughes in the Hispanic World and Haiti* (Hamden, Conn.: Archon Books, 1977); Martha K. Cobb, *Harlem, Haiti, and Havana: A Comprehensive Study of Langston Hughes, Jacques Roumain, and Nicholas Guillén* (Washington, D.C.: Three Continents Press, 1979).

8. Countee Cullen, "Poet on Poet," *Opportunity* 4 (4 March 1926): 73-74.

9. Blyden Jackson, "Langston Hughes," in *Black American Writers: Bibliographical Essays*, ed. M. Thomas Inge, Maurice Duke, and Jackson Bryer (New York: St Martin's Press, 1978), 1:194, asks for more scholarly work on the dramas.

CHAPTER 1. "FOR A MOMENT I WONDERED"

This chapter is dedicated to Charles H. Nichols.

1. W.E.B. Du Bois, *A Soliloquy on Viewing My Life from the Last Decade of Its First Century* (n.p.: International Publishers, 1968) 12-13.

2. WF, 32. Cleanth Brooks and Robert Penn Warren, eds., *Understanding Poetry* (1938; New York: Holt, 1960); W.K. Wimsatt, *The Verbal Icon* (Lexington: Univ. Press of Kentucky, 1954).

3. Dickinson, *Bio-Bibliography*, 103.

4. Consider the thoughtful statement and revision in Langston Hughes, "First Great Poetic Friend [Lincoln] of Letters," *Chicago Defender*, 4 July 1953; and idem, "Like Whitman, Great Artists Are Not Always Good People," *Chicago Defender*, 1 Aug. 1953. See also "Old Walt," in *SP*, 100; Donald B. Gibson, "The Good Black Poet and the Good Gray Poet: The Poetry of Hughes and Whitman," in O'Daniel, *Langston Hughes*, 65-80 (reprinted in Gibson, ed., *Modern Black Poets* [Englewood Cliffs, N.J.: Prentice-Hall, 1973], 43-56).

5. Patricia E. Taylor, "Langston Hughes and the Harlem Renais-

sance, 1921-1931: Major Events and Publications," in *The Harlem Renaissance Remembered*, ed. Arna Bontemps (New York: Dodd, Mead, 1972), 90.

6. Ibid., 98.

7. Dickinson, *Bio-Bibliography*, 60.

8. Langston Hughes, "The Negro Mother," in *The Negro Mother and Other Dramatic Recitations* (New York: Golden Stair Press, 1931), 1; *SP*, 288-89.

9. Milton Rugoff, *Booklist*, October 1, 1940, p. 34.

10. George E. Kent, "Preface: Gwen's Way," in *Report from Part One* (Detroit, Mich.: Broadside Press, 1972), 35.

11. Berry, *Langston Hughes*, 184; Rampersad, *Life* 1:264-65, 286-88.

12. I am grateful to the curators of the Vivian G. Harsh Collection, in the Carter G. Woodson Branch of the Chicago Public Library, and to the late George E. Kent for encouraging me to review the three drafts and the galleys of *The Big Sea*.

13. En route to Spain in July 1937, Hughes attended the Second International Writers' Congress in Paris as a famous poet and revolutionary who had been denied Spanish visas and press credentials by the U.S. State Department. At the closing session on 17 July, when he voiced his anger at the British (for the seizure of Raj Anand's passport) and at the fascists in no uncertain terms, he got a standing ovation. Eventually, he crossed the French border into Spain, wangling his press credentials indirectly. In Spain he met Ernest Hemingway and teamed up with the Cuban poet Nicholás Guillén to investigate the war. In addition to journalism, he wrote a number of poems in the heat of events, among them "Air Raid: Barcelona," "Moonlight in Valencia: Civil War," and "Madrid—1937." In a series of twenty-two articles he took up the banner of the International Brigade. He also began translating Garcia Lorca's *Gypsy Ballads* and *Blood Wedding*.

CHAPTER 2. THE "CRYSTAL STAIR" WITHIN

This chapter is dedicated to Jessica Garris Miller.

1. Langston Hughes, "Fancy Free," in *Simple Takes a Wife* (New York: Simon & Schuster, 1953), 80-84.

2. Maud Bodkin, *Archetypal Patterns in Poetry* (New York: Oxford Univ. Press, 1934) 165. In discussing transformational archetype, I am

combining the literary theories of Bodkin with the linguistic theories of Noam Chomsky: see John Lyons, *Noam Chomsky* (New York: Viking Press, 1970).

3. See Emanuel, *Langston Hughes*. "Mother to Son," *Crisis*, Dec. 1922, p. 87, appears also in *WB*, 107, and in *SP*, 187.

4. See, e.g., Henderson, *Understanding the New Black Poetry*.

5. In the controversial but intriguing study *Black English* (New York: Vintage Books, 1972), J.L. Dillard makes the perceptive distinction that a speaker of standard English must make the tense but can choose "to indicate or to ignore the ongoing or static quality of an action. On the contrary, Black English gives the speaker an option in regard to tense, but its rules demand that the speaker commit himself as to whether the action was continuous or momentary." In "Mother to Son" the action is continuous.

6. See "Cora Unashamed," in *WF*, 3-18; and "Father and Son," *WF*, 200-248. It is intriguing that Cora both opens and closes *White Folks* in part, and someone needs to study her presence as the sign of human possibility and Black experience in the shaping of Langston Hughes' literary world.

7. "Down Where I Am," *PL*, 50. In the 1940s and afterward, his mythic image weakens drastically or even disappears. We find, then, a collapse of the cosmic order that once characterized his poetic world. Many observers have implied the trend: Owen Dodson, "Shakespeare in Harlem," *Phylon II* (1942): 332-38; Theodore R. Hudson, "Langston Hughes' Last Volume of Verse," *CLA Journal* 11 (1968): 280-90; Gibson, "Good Black Poet."

8. Langston Hughes, *One-Way Ticket* (New York: Knopf, 1949); and *SP*, 201-18.

9. See Gibson, "Good Black Poet"; Ken Peeples, Jr., "The Paradox of the 'Good Gray' Poet [Walt Whitman] on Slavery and the Black Man," *Phylon* 35 (1974).

10. Wallace Stevens, "Sunday Morning," in *Poems* (New York: Viking Press, 1974), 5.

11. See, esp. "The Waste Land" and "Ash Wednesday" in T.S. Eliot, *Selected Poems* (New York: Harcourt, Brace & World, 1930). In the former, one can interpret the cry of the bartender at the end of Part II, "A Game of Chess," as requesting redemption from the godless maze of twentieth-century existence. In climaxing a portrait of infidelity, the ending of Part III, "A Fire Sermon," reinforces the theme

of redemption: "O Lord Thou pluckest me out." In the opening section of "Ash Wednesday," the narrative "I" hopes calmly and repetitiously for the redemption rather than demanding it: "Pray for us sinners now and at the hour of our death / Pray for us now and at the hour of our death."

12. See Alan Ginsberg, "America," in *The New Modern Poetry*, ed. M.L. Rosenthal (New York: Oxford Univ. Press, 1967), 67-70.

CHAPTER 3. "DEEP LIKE THE RIVERS"

1. W.R. Johnson, *The Idea of Lyric* (Berkeley: Univ. of California Press, 1982), 23.

2. See R. Baxter Miller, " 'A Mere Poem': 'Daybreak in Alabama,' Resolution to Langston Hughes's Commentary on Music and Art," *Obsidian* 2 (1976): 30-37.

3. See Gibson, "Good Black Poet," 65-80.

4. See *The Philosophy of Edmund Burke*, ed. Louis T. Bredvold and Ralph G. Ross (Ann Arbor: Univ. of Michigan, 1967), 256-67.

5. See Felix E. Schelling, *The English Lyric* (Boston: Houghton Mifflin, 1913), 1-2; Barbara Hardy, *The Advantage of Lyric* (Bloomington: Indiana Univ. Press, 1977), 1-3.

6. The position disagrees with Schelling's.

7. The distinction is Johnson's, *Idea of Lyric*.

8. Ibid., 23.

9. Ibid.

10. Ruth Finnegan, *Oral Poetry* (London: Cambridge Univ. Press, 1977), 25-29; Thomas R. Edwards, *Imagination and Power: A Study of Poetry of Public Themes* (New York: Oxford Univ. Press, 1971), 6.

11. Denis Donoghue, *The Sovereign Ghost* (Berkeley: Univ. of California Press, 1976), 221-22.

12. Ibid., 228.

13. Seiichi Hatano, *Time and Eternity*, trans. Ichiro Suzuki (Japan: Ministry of Education, 1963), 20.

14. Hatano *Time and Eternity*, 148.

15. See Levi, *Literature, Philosophy, and the Imagination*, 274.

16. See Peter Conrad, *Imagining America* (New York: Oxford Univ. Press, 1980), 5.

17. See Berry, *Langston Hughes*, 61.

18. I am considering poems here, however, in terms of their actual appearance within the overall structure of *Weary Blues*.

19. See Chancellor Williams, *The Destruction of Black Civilization* (Chicago: Third World Press, 1976), 139.

20. "Home," the metaphor of death, occurs in the play *Soul Gone Home*"; see *Five Plays by Langston Hughes*, ed. Webster Smalley (Bloomington: Indiana Univ. Press, 1963).

21. Jemie, *Langston Hughes*, 139.

22. See Johnson, *Idea of Lyric*, 1, 23.

23. See Arthur P. Davis, "Langston Hughes: Cool Poet," *CLA Journal* 11 (June 1968): 276-83.

24. Donoghue, *Sovereign Ghost*, 224-25.

25. Though Gibson ("Good Black Poet") deals satisfactorily with the sources in Whitman, nearly everyone overlooks the Victorians, perhaps because such a wide chasm separates their aesthetic, moral, and social sensibilities from those of Hughes.

26. SP, 100; originally published in *Beloit Poetry Journal*, no. 5 (1954): 10.

27. For a folk reading, see Richard K. Barksdale, "Langston Hughes: His Times and Humanistic Techniques," in *Black American Literature and Humanism*, ed. R. Baxter Miller (Lexington: Univ. Press of Kentucky, 1981), 23-25.

28. Johnson, *Idea of Lyric*, 195.

29. Apparently the theme appealed to Hughes; both stories appear in Langston Hughes, ed., *The Best Short Stories by Negro Writers* (Boston: Little, Brown, 1967), 130-33, 490-96.

30. "Black Maria," *Poetry*, (May 1941), pp. 74-75; SP, 118.

CHAPTER 4. "OH, MIND OF MAN"

This chapter is dedicated to George H. Bass.

1. "History," *Opportunity* 16 (Nov. 1934): 339; NS, 19; PL, 69.

2. David Kenneth Fieldhouse, *Colonialism, 1870-1945: An Introduction* (New York: St. Martin's Press, 1981), 396-400; Robert J. McMahon, *Colonialism and Cold War* (Ithaca: Cornell Univ. Press, 1981); Raymond F. Betts, *The False Dawn: European Imperialism in the Nineteenth Century* (Minneapolis: Univ. of Minnesota Press, 1975), 216; Geoffrey Barraclough, *An Introduction to Contemporary History* (Baltimore, Md.: Penguin, 1967), 153. Chester J. Fontenot, Jr., *Franz Fanon:*

Language as the God Gone Astray in the Flesh, University of Nebraska Studies, New Series No. 60 (Lincoln, Neb.: Board of Regents, 1979).

3. Rosalind Coward and John Ellis, *Language and Materialism: Developments in Semiology and the Theories of the Subject* (Boston: Routledge & Kegan Paul, 1977), 72.

4. See Kinfe Abraham, *From Race to Class: Links and Parallels in African and Black American Protest Expression* (London: Grassroots Publishers, 1982).

5. "October 16," *Opportunity* 9 (Oct. 1931): 299; JC, 14; One-Way Ticket, 89-90; SP, 10; *La Procellaria,* Sept.-Oct. 1961, p. 42; cited here from PL, 28-29.

6. But they speak in code.

7. "A New Song," *Opportunity* 11 (Jan. 1933): 23; Crisis, 40 (March 1933): 59; NS, 24-25.

8. Kramaya, 4 Nov. 1933; JC, 20; SP, 238-39.

9. Crisis, March 1940; JC, 24; SP, 190.

10. See Barksdale, "Langston Hughes," 19-21.

11. Gwendolyn Brooks, "Langston Hughes," in *Selected Poems* (New York: Harper & Row, 1963), 123. See R. Baxter Miller, "The Humanistic Aesthetic of Gwendolyn Brooks," in Miller, *Black American Literature,* 106-7.

12. Berry, *Langston Hughes,* 301-2.

13. Unquote, June 1940; JC, 25; SP, 157; PL, 101.

14. Arna Bontemps, a writer in the naturalistic mode, values the poem considerably less highly. See Charles H. Nichols, ed., *Arna Bontemps–Langston Hughes Letters, 1925-1967* (New York: Dodd, Mead, 1980).

15. To avoid distortion of Hughes' own imaginative ordering of the poems within the individual volumes published in his lifetime (and he often revised and republished the same poem), I consider the previously uncollected writings from *Good Morning Revolution* in this separate section rather than in a strictly chronological order integrated with that of the other texts.

16. His own skillful lyrics implicitly contradicted such skepticism throughout his lifetime.

17. Despite his brilliance as a definitive biographer of Langston Hughes, I must differ here with my colleague Arnold Rampersad, who writes: "In spite of [its] hostility, however, and perhaps the poorest sales of any book Hughes would ever publish (a fact he attributed to

its title), *Fine Clothes to the Jew* was also his most brilliant book of poems, and one of the more astonishing books of verse ever published in the United States—comparable in the black world to *Leaves of Grass* in the white" (*Life of Langston Hughes,* 1:141).

18. "Cultural Exchange" (AYM, 3-9) is most accessible perhaps in Dudley Randall, *The Black Poets* (New York: Bantam Books, 1971), 83-84, and in *PL,* 81-83. It is cited here from the typescript on file at the Lilly Library, Indiana University.

19. Peter M. Bergman and Mort N. Bergman, *The Chronological History of the Negro in America* (New York: New American Library, 1969), 296, 451.

20. " 'You are saved: what has cast such a shadow upon you?' 'The Negro' ": Herman Melville, "Benito Cereno," in *Billy Budd and Other Tales* (New York: New American Library, 1961), based on the text edited by Frederick Barron Freeman, corrected by Elizabeth Treeman © President and Fellows of Harvard College, in 1948).

21. My observations on *Panther* involve the degree to which the twenty-six poems drawn from previous books appear in a new light and tone in conjunction with the forty-four new ones. Of primary concern are the divisions headed Words on Fire, American Heartbreak, Bible Belt, and Face of War.

22. Only Hughes and his mentor, Du Bois, seem to have been so prophetic.

23. Robert B. Stepto, *From Behind the Veil: A Study of Afro-American Narrative* (Urbana: Univ. of Illinois, 1979).

CHAPTER 5. "I HEARD MA RAINEY"

This chapter is dedicated to Blyden Jackson.

1. Performed by the Gilpin Players at Karamu House, Cleveland, Ohio, December 1936. Script in the James Weldon Johnson Collection, Beinecke Rare Book and Manuscript Library, Yale University. Darwin T. Turner, in "Langston Hughes as Playwright," writes as follows:

Throughout his professional writing career of forty-six years Langston Hughes maintained keen interest in theater. He published his first play, *The Gold Piece,* in 1921. In 1935, he had his first Broadway show—*Mulatto,* which established a record by remaining in production on Broadway longer than any other play which had been written by a Negro. During the thirties and early forties, he founded three Negro dramatic groups—the Suitcase Theater in Harlem, the Negro Art Theater in Los Angeles, and the Skyloft Players in Chicago. As late as 1963, Hughes was still polishing *Emperor of Haiti*, which had been produced as *Drums of Haiti* twenty-seven years earlier. [81]

Emperor of Haiti is the story of Jean Jacques Dessalines' progress from slave to emperor to corpse. Beginning during the Haitian blacks' rebellion against their French masters and treating historical fact freely, the play focuses the economic and personal problems of Dessalines' rule as emperor. Economically, the kingdom suffers because Dessalines refuses to require labor from the liberated blacks. When he finally realizes the need, they turn against him. Personally, Dessalines fails in Hughes's play because, after becoming emperor, he rejects his uneducated wife Azelea, who loves him. In her place, he takes Claire Heureuse, a pawn of the mulattoes who seek to overthrow him. The play climaxes and ends when, riding to crush a rebellion, Dessalines is killed in the trap set by mulattoes. Melodramatically, Azelea, now a penniless street seller, discovers his body and mourns his death while Claire flees with her mulatto lover, and two passing Haitians fail to recognize their emperor. [94]

2. Langston Hughes, "Troubled Island: Story of Dreams, Tragedy," *Chicago Defender*, 2 April 1949, p. 6.

3. George Steiner, *The Death of Tragedy* (1961; New York: Oxford Univ. Press, 1980), 354.

4. Maurice Charney, *Comedy High and Low: An Introduction to the Experience of Comedy* (New York: Oxford Univ. Press, 1978), 87. Charney considers the principles of comedy as well on pp. 11, 59, 69, 72, 77, 80, 82, 94, 97, 106, 152, 173.

5. Ibid., 11. See also Lamine Diarkhaté, "Langston Hughes, conquérant de l'espoir," *Présence Africaine* 64 (1967): 38-46; and François Dodat, "Situation de Langston Hughes," *Présence Africaine* 64 (1967): 47-50.

6. Charney, *Comedy*, 175.

7. "Berry," *Abbott's Weekly*, 24 Feb. 1935; reprinted in WF, 171-82.

8. See Bergman and Bergman, *Chronological History*, 453.

9. See James A. Emanuel, "The Literary Experiments of Langston Hughes," *CLA Journal* 11 (1968): 335-44.

10. Contrary to some opinion, Hughes himself did not incarnate such a trend. See Elizabeth Staples, "Langston Hughes: Malevolent Force," *American Mercury* 88 (1959): 46-50.

11. Steiner, *Death of Tragedy*, 354.

12. Langston Hughes, "Big Round World," in *Simple Stakes a Claim* (New York: Rinehart, 1957), 23-28. The tales cited are chosen deliberately from the middle, early, and final periods in Hughes' treatment of Simple.

13. Charney, *Comedy*, 52.

14. Ibid., 72-73.

15. Langston Hughes, "Shadow of the Blues," in *Simple Takes a Wife* (New York: Simon & Schuster, 1953) 172-75.

16. Langston Hughes, "Lynn Clarisse," in *Simple's Uncle Sam* (New York: Hill & Wang, 1965), 83-86.

17. Charney, *Comedy*, 90. Langston Hughes had written about Blacks in the *Chicago Defender*, 2 Oct. 1948, p. 1: "Maybe it is this very laughter that has kept us going all these years, from slavery's denial of the drought of freedom up to the Washington airport's denial of work. Maybe it is just a way of saying, 'To defeat us, you must defeat our laughter.' "

18. Berry, *Langston Hughes*, 329.

SELECTED BIBLIOGRAPHY

PRIMARY SOURCES: WORKS BY LANGSTON HUGHES

Books

The Weary Blues. New York: Knopf, 1926.

Fine Clothes to the Jew. New York: Knopf, 1927.

Not With Laughter. New York: Knopf, 1930; London: Allen & Unwin, 1930.

Dear Lovely Death. Amenia, N.Y.: Troutbeck Press, 1931 (privately printed).

The Negro Mother and Other Dramatic Recitations. New York: Golden Stair Press, 1931.

The Dream Keeper and Other Poems. New York: Knopf, 1932.

Scottsboro Limited: Four Poems and a Play in Verse. New York: Golden Stair Press, 1932.

Popo and Fifina: Children of Haiti. With Arna Bontemps. New York: Macmillan, 1932.

A Negro Looks at Soviet Central Asia. Moscow: Co-operative Publishing Society of Foreign Workers in the U.S.S.R., 1934.

The Ways of White Folks. New York: Knopf, 1934; London: Allen & Unwin, 1934.

A New Song. New York: International Workers Order, 1938.

The Big Sea: An Autobiography. New York: Knopf, 1940; London: Hutchinson, 1940.

Shakespeare in Harlem. New York: Knopf, 1942.

Freedom's Plow. New York: Musette, 1943.

Jim Crow's Last Stand. Atlanta, Ga.: Negro Publication Society of America, 1943.

Lament for Dark Peoples and Other Poems. N.p., 1944.

Fields of Wonder. New York: Knopf, 1947.

One-Way Ticket. New York: Knopf, 1949.

Troubled Island. Opera libretto, music by William Grant Still. New York: Leeds Music, 1949.

Simple Speaks His Mind. New York: Simon & Schuster, 1950; London: Gollancz, 1951.

Montage of a Dream Deferred. New York: Holt, 1951.

Laughing to Keep from Crying. New York: Holt, 1952.

The First Book of Negroes. New York: Franklin Watts, 1952; London: Bailey & Swinfen, 1956.

Simple Takes a Wife. New York: Simon & Schuster, 1953; London: Gollancz, 1954.

The Glory round His Head. Libretto, music by Jan Meyerowitz. New York: Broude Brothers, 1953.

Famous American Negroes. New York: Dodd, Mead, 1954.

The First Book of Rhythms. New York: Franklin Watts, 1954; London: Bailey & Swinfen, 1956.

The First Book of Jazz. New York: Franklin Watts, 1955; London: Bailey & Swinfen, 1957.

Famous Negro Music Makers. New York: Dodd, Mead, 1955.

The Sweet Flypaper of Life. Photo essay, photographs by Roy DeCarava New York: Simon & Schuster, 1955.

The First Book of the West Indies. New York: Franklin Watts, 1956; London: Bailey & Swinfen, 1956. Republished as *The First Book of the Caribbean* (London: Edmund Ward, 1965).

I Wonder as I Wander: An Autobiographical Journey. New York: Rinehart, 1956.

A Pictorial History of the Negro in America. With Milton Meltzer New York: Crown, 1956; rev. eds. 1963, 1968. Revised as *A Pictorial History of Black Americans,* with Meltzer and C. Eric Lincoln (New York: Crown, 1973).

Simple Stakes a Claim. New York: Rinehart, 1957; London: Gollancz, 1958.

The Langston Hughes Reader. New York: Braziller, 1958.

Famous Negro Heroes of America. New York: Dodd, Mead, 1958.

Tambourines to Glory. New York; John Day, 1958; London: Gollancz, 1959.

Selected Poems of Langston Hughes. New York: Knopf, 1959.

Simply Heavenly. Book and lyrics, music by David Martin. New York: Dramatists Play Service, 1959.

The First Book of Africa. New York: Franklin Watts, 1960; London: Mayflower, 1961; rev. ed. 1964.

The Best of Simple. New York: Hill & Wang, 1961.

Ask Your Mama: 12 Moods for Jazz. New York: Knopf, 1961.

The Ballad of the Brown King. Cantata libretto, music by Margaret Bonds. New York: Sam Fox, 1961.

Fight for Freedom: The Story of the NAACP. New York: Norton, 1962.

Something in Common and Other Stories. New York: Hill & Wang, 1963.

Five Plays by Langston Hughes. Ed. Webster Smalley. Bloomington: Indiana Univ. Press, 1963.

Simple's Uncle Sam. New York: Hill & Wang, 1965.

The Panther and The Lash: Poems of Our Times. New York: Knopf, 1967.

Black Magic: A Pictorial History of the Negro in American Entertainment. With Milton Meltzer. Englewood Cliffs, N.J.: Prentice-Hall, 1967.

Black Misery. New York: Knopf, 1969.

Good Morning Revolution: Uncollected Social Protest Writings by Langston Hughes. Ed. Faith Berry. New York: Lawrence Hill, 1973.

Arna Bontemps–Langston Hughes Letters, 1925-1967. Ed. Charles H. Nichols. New York: Dodd, Mead, 1980.

First Productions of Plays

Mulatto. New York, Vanderbilt Theatre, 24 October 1935.

Little Ham. Cleveland, Karamu House, March 1936.

When the Jack Hollers. With Arna Bontemps. Cleveland, Karamu House, April 1936.

Troubled Island. Cleveland, Karamu House, December 1936; opera version with music by William Grant Still, New York City Center, 31 March 1949.

Joy to My Soul. Cleveland, Karamu House, March 1937.

Soul Gone Home. Cleveland Federal Theatre, 1937.

Don't You Want to be Free? New York, Harlem Suitcase Theatre, 21 April 1938.

Front Porch. Cleveland, Karamu House, November 1938.

The Organizer. With music by James P. Johnson, New York, Harlem Suitcase Theatre, March 1939.

The Sun Do Move. Chicago, Good Shepherd Community House, Spring 1942.

Street Scene. lyrics. Book by Elmer Rice, music by Kurt Weill. New York, Adelphi Theatre, 9 January 1947.

The Barrier. With music by Jan Meyerowitz. New York, Columbia University, January 1950; New York, Broadhurst Theatre, 2 November 1950.

Just Around the Corner. lyrics. Book by Amy Mann and Bernard Drew, music by Joe Sherman. Ogunguit, Maine, Playhouse, Summer 1951.

Esther. With music by Jan Meyerowitz. Urbana, University of Illinois, March 1957.

Simply Heavenly. New York, Eighty-fifth Street Playhouse, 20 October 1957.

The Ballad of the Brown King. With music by Margaret Bonds. New York City YMCA, Clark Auditorium, 11 December 1960.

Black Nativity. New York, Forty-first Street Theatre, 11 December 1961.

Gospel Glow. Brooklyn, New York, Washington Temple, October 1962.

Tambourines to Glory. New York, Little Theatre, 2 November 1963.

Let Us Remember Him. With music by David Amram. San Francisco, War Memorial Opera House, 15 November 1963.

Jerico-Jim Crow. New York, Village Presbyterian Church and Brotherhood Synagogue, 28 December 1964.

The Prodigal Son. New York, Greenwich Mews Theatre, 20 May 1965.

Miscellaneous Poems

The New Negro. Ed. Alain Locke. Includes nine poems by Hughes. New York: A. & C. Boni, 1925.

Four Negro Poets. New York: Simon & Schuster, 1927. Includes twenty-one poems by Hughes.

Four Lincoln University Poets. Lincoln, Pa.: Lincoln University Herald, 1930. Includes six poems by Hughes.

Elmer Rice and Kurt Weill, *Street Scene.* New York: Chappell, 1948. Lyrics by Hughes.

Editions

The Poetry of the Negro, 1746-1949. Ed. with Arna Bontemps. Garden City, N.Y.: Doubleday, 1949.

Lincoln University Poets. Ed. with Waring Cuney, and Bruce McM. Wright. New York: Fine Editions Press, 1954.

The Book of Negro Folklore. Ed. with Arna Bontemps. New York: Dodd, Mead, 1958.

An African Treasury: Articles/Essays/Stories/Poems by Black Americans. With introduction by Hughes. New York: Crown, 1960; London: Gollancz, 1961.

Poems From Black Africa. Bloomington: Indiana Univ. Press, 1963.

New Negro Poets: U.S.A. Bloomington: Indiana Univ. Press, 1964.

The Book of Negro Humor. New York: Dodd, Mead, 1966.

The Best Short Stories by Negro Writers. Edited, with an introduction, by Hughes. Boston: Little, Brown, 1967.

Translations

Federico Garcia Lorca, *San Gabriel.* N.p., 1938.

Jacques Roumain, "When the Tom-Tom Beats" and "Guinea"; Refino Pedroso, "Opinions of the New Chinese Student." In *Anthology of Contemporary Latin-American Poetry,* ed. Dudley Fitts, 191-93, 247-49. Norfolk, Conn.: New Directions, 1942.

Jacques Roumain, *Masters of the Dew.* Trans. with Mercer Cook. New York: Reynal & Hitchcock, 1947.

Nicolas Guillén, *Cuba Libre.* Trans. with Ben Frederic Carruthers. Los Angeles: Ward Richie Press, 1948.

Leon Damas, "Really I Know," "Trite without Doubt," and "She Left Herself One Evening." In *The Poetry of the Negro, 1746-1949,* 371-72. Garden City, N.Y.: Doubleday, 1949.

Federico Garcia Lorca, *Gypsy Ballads.* Beloit Poetry Chap-book, no. 1. Beloit, Wis.: Beloit Poetry Journal, 1951.

Gabriela Mistral (Lucila Godoy Alcayaga), *Selected Poems.* Bloomington: Indiana Univ. Press, 1957.

Jean-Joseph Rabearivelo, "Flute Players"; David Diop, "Those Who Lost Everything" and "Suffer, Poor Negro." In *Poems from Black Africa,* 131-32, 143-45. Bloomington: Indiana Univ. Press, 1963.

SECONDARY SOURCES AND BIBLIOGRAPHIES

Barksdale, Richard K. "Langston Hughes: His Times and His Humanistic Techniques." In *Black American Literature and Humanism*, ed. R. Baxter Miller, 11-26. Lexington: Univ. Press of Kentucky, 1981.
———. *Langston Hughes: The Poet and His Critics*. Chicago: American Library Association, 1977. [with bibliography]
Bass, George Houston. "Five Stories about a Man Named Hughes: A Critical Reflection." *Langston Hughes Review* 1 (1982): 1-12.
Berry, Faith. *Langston Hughes: Before and Beyond Harlem*. Westport, Conn.: Lawrence Hill, 1983.
Black American Literature Forum 15 (1981). Special Hughes issue, ed. R. Baxter Miller.
Brown, Lloyd W. "The Portrait of the Artist as a Black American in the Poetry of Langston Hughes." *Studies in Black Literature* 5 (1974): 24-27.
Brown, Soi-Daniel W. " 'Black Orpheus': Langston Hughes' Reception in German Translation (An Overview)." *Langston Hughes Review* 4 (1985): 30-38.
Cobb, Martha K. "Concepts of Blackness in the Poetry of Nicholas Guillén, Jacques Roumain, and Langston Hughes." *CLA Journal* 18 (1975): 262-72.
Davis, Arthur P. *From the Dark Tower: Afro-American Writers from 1900-1960*. Washington, D.C.: Howard Univ. Press, 1974. [with bibliography]
———. "Langston Hughes: Cool Poet." *CLA Journal* 11 (1968): 280-96.
———. "The Tragic Mulatto Theme in Six Works by Langston Hughes." *Phylon* 16 (1955): 195-204. Reprinted in *Five Black Writers*, ed. Donald B. Gibson (New York: New York Univ. Press, 1970), 167-77. [with bibliography]
Dickinson, Donald C. *A Bio-Bibliography of Langston Hughes, 1902-1967*. Hamden, Conn.: Shoe String Press, 1967.
Du Bois, W.E.B., and Alain Locke. "The Younger Literary Movement." *Crisis* 27 (1927): 161-63.
Emanuel, James. *Langston Hughes*. New York: Twayne, 1967. [with bibliography]
———. "The Literary Experiments of Langston Hughes." *CLA Journal* 11 (1967): 335-44.

Filatova, Lydia. "Langston Hughes: American Writer." *International Literature* 1 (1933): 103-5.

Gates, Skip. "Of Negroes Old and New." *Transition* 46 (n.d.): 44-57.

Gayle, Addison. "Langston Hughes: A Simple Commentary." *Negro Digest* 16 (1967): 53-57.

Gibson, Donald B. "The Good Black Poet and the Good Gray Poet: The Poetry of Hughes and Whitman." In *Langston Hughes: Black Genius*, ed. Therman B. O'Daniel, 65-80. New York: Morrow, 1971.

——. ed. *Five Black Writers: Essays on Wright, Ellison, Baldwin, Hughes, and LeRoi Jones*. New York: New York Univ. Press, 1970.

Govan, Sandra. "The Poetry of the Black Experience as Counterpoint to the Poetry of the Black Aesthetic." *Negro American Literature Forum* 8 (1975): 288-92.

Guillaume, Alfred, Jr. "And Bid Him Translate: Langston Hughes' Translation of Poetry from French." *Langston Hughes Review* 4 (1985): 1-8.

Hudson, Theodore. "Langston Hughes' Last Volume of Verse." *CLA Journal* 11 (1968): 345-48.

Huggins, Nathan. *Harlem Renaissance*. New York: Oxford Univ. Press, 1971.

Jackson, Blyden. "A Word about Simple." *CLA Journal* 11 (1968): 310-18.

Jemie, Onwuchekwa. *Langston Hughes: An Introduction to the Poetry*. New York: Columbia Univ. Press, 1976.

Jones, Harry L. "Simple Speaks Spanish." *Langston Hughes Review* 4 (1985): 24-26.

Kearney, Reginald. "Langston Hughes in Japanese Translation." *Langston Hughes Review* 4 (1985): 27-29.

Kent, George. "Langston Hughes and the Afro-American Folk and Cultural Tradition." In *Langston Hughes: Black Genius*, ed. Therman B. O'Daniel, 183-210. New York: Morrow, 1971.

Killens, John. "Broadway in Black and White." *African Forum* 1 (n.d.): 66-76.

King, Woodie. "Remembering Langston Hughes." *Negro Digest* 18 (1969): 27-32, 95-96.

Kinnamon, Keneth. "The Man Who Created Simple." *Nation* 205 (1967): 599-601.

Kramer, Aaron. "Robert Burns and Langston Hughes." *Freedomways* 8 (1968): 159-66.

Lash, John S. "The American Negro and American Literature: A Checklist of Significant Commentaries." *Bulletin of Bibliography* 19 ( ): 12-15, 33-36.

Lewis, David Levering. *When Harlem Was in Vogue.* New York: Knopf, 1981.

Locke, Alain. "The Negro in American Culture." In *Anthology of American Negro Literature,* ed. V.F. Calverton. New York: Modern Library, 1929.

———, ed. "The Negro Poets of the United States." In *Anthology of Magazine Verse for 1926, and Yearbook of Poetry,* ed. William Stanley Braithwaite. Boston: B.J. Brimmer, 1927.

Mandelik, Peter, and Stanley Schatt. *Concordance to Langston Hughes.* Detroit, Mich.: Gale Research, 1975.

Matheus, John F. "Langston Hughes as Translator." *CLA Journal* 11 (1968): 319-30.

Miller, R. Baxter. "For a Moment I Wondered: Theory and Form in the Autobiographies of Langston Hughes." *Langston Hughes Review* 3 (1984): 1-6.

———. *Langston Hughes and Gwendolyn Brooks: A Reference Guide.* Boston: G.K. Hall, 1978.

Mitchell, Loften. *Black Drama: The Story of the American Negro in the Theatre.* New York: Hawthorne Books, 1967.

Mullen, Edward, ed. *Critical Essays on Langston Hughes.* Boston: G.K. Hall, 1986.

O'Daniel, Therman B., ed. *Langston Hughes: Black Genius.* New York: Morrow, 1971.

Osofsky, Gilbert. "Symbols of the Jazz Age: The New Negro and Harlem Discovered." *American Quarterly* 17 (1966): 229-36.

Parker, John W. "Tomorrow in the Writing of Langston Hughes." *College English* 10 (1949): 438-41.

Patterson, Lindsay. "Langston Hughes—An Inspirer of Young Writers." *Freedomways* 8 (1968): 179-81.

Patterson, Louise. "With Langston Hughes in the USSR." *Freedomways* 8 (1968): 152-58.

Pool, Rosey. "The Discovery of American Negro Poetry." *Freedomways* 3 (1963): 511-17.

Presley, James. "The American Dream of Langston Hughes." *Southwest Review* 48 (1948): 380-86.

Rampersad, Arnold. *The Life of Langston Hughes*. 2 vols. New York: Oxford Univ. Press, 1986, 1988.

Redding, Saunders. *To Make a Poet Black*. Chapel Hill: Univ. of North Carolina Press, 1939.

Rollins, Charlemae. *Black Troubador: Langston Hughes*. Chicago: Rand McNally, 1970.

Schatt, Stanley. "Langston Hughes: The Minstrel as Artificer." *Journal of Modern Literature* 4 (1974): 115-20.

Smalley, Webster, ed. *Five Plays by Langston Hughes*. Bloomington: Indiana Univ. Press, 1963.

Staples, Elizabeth. "Langston Hughes: Malevolent Force." *American Mercury* 98 (1959): 46-50.

Thurman, Wallace. "Negro Artists and the Negro." *New Republic* 52 (1928): 37-39.

Turner, Darwin T. "Langston Hughes as Playwright." *CLA Journal* 11 (1968): 297-309.

Turpin, Waters E. "Four Short Fiction Writers of the Harlem Renaissance—Their Legacy of Achievement." *CLA Journal* 11 (1968): 59-72.

Wagner, Jean. "Langston Hughes." In *Black Poets of the United States*, trans. Kenneth Douglass, 385-474. Urbana: Univ. of Illinois Press, 1973.

Walker, Margaret. "New Poets." *Phylon* 11 (1950): 345-54.

INDEX

"Advertisement for Opening of the Waldorf-Astoria," 24
Alianza de Intelectuales, 30
American civilization, struggle of humanity in, 69
American Dream, 121
Anand, Raj, 127 n 13
Apartheid, in South Africa, 96, 111
artist, fallen, 28
"As I Grew Older," 54
Ask Your Mama, 69, 71; dream and social injustice in, 31; memory and human consciousness shaped through words, 68; neglected brilliance of, 85-94
Association for the Study of Negro Life and History, 16
Atlantic Monthly, 18
"Aunt Sue's Stories," 25, 41
autobiographical self: failure to create, 23; invisibility of, 22. See also narrative self
Autobiography of Malcolm X, 20

Baker, Josephine, 14
"Ballad of the Landlord," 5, 75, 120

Bass, George H., 130
Before the Mayflower, 15
"Benito Cereno," 132 n 20
Bennett, Lerone, Jr., 15
Bentley, Gladys, 17
Berry, Faith, 120
"Berry," 103-04
Bethune, Mary McLeod, 18, 19
"Big Round World," 110-12
"Big Sea, The," 6, 9, 28-32; record of milestones, 121
"Bitter River, The," 77
Black American Dream, 4
Black art: corruption of, 26; as sublimation, 74
Black Manhattan, 15
Black middle class, 14
Black panthers, 95
Black woman, 33-46; folk source, 33; heroic determination of, 33; literary imagination, 121; sources in and development of, 121; as spiritual figure, 124; types of, 41
Bledsoe, Jules, 15
Blood Wedding, 127 n 13
"Blue Bayou," 76

Blues: and death, 7; as reaffirmation
of human spirit, 114; as transcen-
dence and defiance, 49-50, 120; as
triumph, 31
"Blues I'm Playing, The," 26
Bodkin, Maud, 34
Bontemps, Arna, 15, 17
Brooks, Gwendolyn, 77
Brown, John, 71, 80, 122
Bryant, William Cullen, 45

cafe: emblem in Paris of order and
art, 1; as haven from historical
time, 116
"Carolina Cabin," 60
Charney, Maurice, 101
Chicago Defender, 119
Christian love: restorative power of,
through storytelling, 103
Christian Register, 59
Christophe, Henri, 99
CLA Journal, 5
Cobb, Martha, 5
Coleridge, Samuel Taylor, 3
colonialism, 68
comedy, artistic control in, 2
"Concerning 'Goodbye Christ,' " 83
"Cora Unashamed," 128 n 6
Cotton Club, 14
Crisis, 5, 25, 34, 49, 56
critical method, 4
"Cross," 49
Cullen, Countee, 17, 48

"Daybreak in Alabama," 21, 34, 48,
123
deconstruction, 5, 28
Dessalines, Jean-Jacques, 99, 118
Dickinson, Donald C., 5, 12, 18
Dillard, J.L., 128 n 4
Divine Mother, 43
Douglas, Aaron, 16
Douglass, Frederick, 22

"Down Where I Am," 33, 43; sign
of declining imagination, 95
dream: fulfillment of, 71; as purity,
75
"Dream Variations," 56
"Drums of Haiti," 133 n 1
Du Bois, W.E.B., 8
Dunbar, Paul Laurence, 48
Duse, Elenora, 31
Dylan, Bob, 52

"Elegy Written in a Country
Churchyard," 58
Eliot, T.S., 45
Ellison, Ralph, 120
Emanuel, James A., 5
Emerson, Ralph Waldo, 45
Emperor Jones, 15
"Emperor of Haiti," 133 n 1
Esquire, 10
Euro-American tradition of poetry,
45

fascism, 79, 83
"Father and Son," 6, 34, 104-09,
128 n 6; tragic death in, 121
Fauset, Jessie, 16
Fields of Wonder, 49, 59-66
Fine Clothes to the Jew, 132 n 17
Fisher, Rudolph, 17-18
Flack, Roberta, 52
folk source, 46
Franklin, John Hope, 15
"Frederick Douglass: 1817-1895," 97
Freedomways, 5
Freudian analysis, 4

Garvey, Marcus, 16
Gilpin Players, 24, 132 n 1
"Gold Piece, The," 132 n 1
"Goodbye Christ," 84
Good Morning Revolution, 68, 131 n
15

Goya, Francisco, 73
great migration, 12
Guillén, Nicholás, 127 n 13
Guthrie, Woody, 52
Gypsy Ballads, 127 n 13

Haiti, 99
Harlem Renaissance, 10, 11, 15
Harlem Renaissance Remembered, 15
Hayes, Roland, 14
Hemingway, Ernest, 127 n 13
history: complex, as embodied
  through woman, 33; contemplative, river as externalized form, 57;
  conversion of political, into personal and racial idiom, 81; linear,
  10; metaphoric code for reading,
  67; mythic, 10; spiraled repetition
  of, 96; tragedy, cycle of, 98
Hitler, Adolph, 30
Holiday, Billie, 49
"Home," 10
Huggins, Nathan, 15
Hughes, Carrie, 14
human conscience, 96
Hurston, Zora Neale, 17-18, 20; and
  controversy over Mule Bone, 24

ideology, humanized and metaphoric, 98
imagination: analogue to race, im-
  posing itself upon history, 43; decline of, "Down where I am," 95;
  dualism of, 52; failure to distill human meaning from despair, 77; literary, definition and historical
  background of, 2-3; Madam's human, 45; poetic, and history, 34;
  in symbolism of light, fire, and
  water, 64; signature upon history,
  59; song as metonym for, 55
—lyrical: freezing of tragic time by,
  47-66, 122; from external landscape to reflective consciousness,
  82; historical background of, 48;
  political excluded from, 81; as
  public performance through, 4; recovery in, 81
—political, 67-98; cyclic, 69; distinguished from lyrical, 67; ebbing
  into lyrical, 81
Invisible Man, 120
I Wonder as I Wander, 1-32

Jackson, Blyden, 132
"Jester," 2, 57
"Jim Crow's Last Stand," 123
Jim Crow's Last Stand, 69, 75, 80-
  82; motif of death and anger in,
  76
Johnson, Charles, 16
Johnson, James Weldon, 15
Johnson, Lemuel, 5
Johnson, W.R., 47

Karamu House, 24, 132 n 1
Kent, George E., 127
"Ku-Klux," 85

Larsen, Nella, 17
laughter, redemptive and historical
  power of, 134 n 17
Lawrence, D.H., 31
Lewis, David Levering, 15
Life and Times of Frederick Douglass,
  The, 20
"Life Is Fine," 25
Lindsay, Vachel, 13, 23, 48, 58
Locke, Alain, 16
Lorca, Federico Garcia, 127 n 13
Louis, Joe, 111
L'Ouverture, Toussaint, 99
Lowell, Amy, 13, 58
Lumumba, Patrice, 70
"Lynn Clarisse," 6, 115-18
lyric awareness: concealed in prose,

9; and frozen moments, 10-11, 29;
and stream of consciousness, 106
See also imagination

"Madam and the Phone Bill," 44
Madam poems, 41-42, 44
Madrid, 31
"Madrid-1937," 33, 73, 82, 123
magical transformation, 110
Marx, Karl, 72, 97, 98
Mason, Mrs. (Charlotte Osgood),
24
Masters, Edgar Lee, 13
Maupassant, Guy de, as literary
source, 11; realism of, 31; revision
of source in, 27, 29
melodramas, 34
Melville, Herman, 132 n 20
"Merry Go Round," 80
metaphor: books as, 31-32; fall of
modern man and American Eden,
31-32; physical and spiritual hunger, 31-32; Odysseus as metonym
for poetic voice, 59; reversal of
darkness and worth of identity, 58;
textual, 55; woman as pervasive
presence, 34; woman as sign of social and personal history, 34
"Mexican Market Woman," 41-42
Miller, Jessica G., 127
Mills, Florence, 13, 14, 16
modernity: illusions displacing pastoral world, 64; placement within,
4
Montage of a Dream Deferred, 59,
120
"Mother to Son," 35-39, 43, 95
"Motto," 59
Mulatto, 24, 34, 51, 52, 104, 105,
132 n 1; tragic death in, 121
Mule Bone, 24
Mullen, Edward J., 5
Murillo, Bratolomé, 73

Mussolini, Benito, 1, 30
Mutter Courage, 109
"My Adventures as a Social Poet,"
85
myth and history, 10; margins of,
61

narrative self: as invisible man, 20;
narrative technique, multiple consciousness, 105; theory of narrative, 20, 21. *See also*
autobiographical self
Negritude, principles of, 11
Negro Art Theater (Los Angeles),
133 n 1
"Negro Mother, The," 35, 41
"Negro Speaks of Rivers, The," 6,
34, 49; explication and reading,
56-57; permanence of memory and
human existence, 51; redemption
through water, 78; starting point
of career, 123
New Masses, 24
New Republic, 12
"New Song," 73
New Song, 71, 73-75
Nichols, Charles H., 126
Not Without Laughter: biographical
source for, 21; publication of, 24

"October 16," 80
O'Daniel, Therman B., 5
"Old Sailor," 61
One-Way Ticket, 6, 25, 34
Opportunity, 5, 16, 54, 57, 80
"Oppression," 49

Pan-Africanism: in Australia, 112;
make-up of, 132 n 21
Panther and the Lash, The, 21, 49,
65
paradox of Harlem Renaissance, 18,
19

Paris: and metaphor of colonialism, 99; on New Year's Eve, 1937-38, 1
Pavón, Pastora, 31
Phylon, 83
"Pierrot," 49
Présence Africaine, 5
psychological criticism, 4

racial discrimination, 13
Rainey, Gertrude "Ma," 98; biography, 115; sign of cultural integrity, history, and conscience, 113-14
Rampersad, Arnold, 5
"Richer, the Poorer, The," 65
Richey, Lionel, 52
ritual, engagement with literary sources and relations, 9
Robeson, Paul, 14
Rose McClendon Players, 14
Roumain, Jacques, 30

Sandburg, Carl, 13
Sano, Seki, 1
Saturday Review, 11, 104
Scribner's Magazine, 26
"Seasape," 59
self and history, 30
"Shadow of the Blues," 6, 112-15; tragic basis of comic laughter in, 115
Shuffle Along, 13
Simone, Nina, 117
Simple, 113; analogy to neoclassic and comic conventions in Shakespeare, 112; comic tales of, 100; as racial chauvinist and universalist, 110; sketches, 6; without middle-class apologies, 115-16
Simple Takes a Wife, 52
"Slave on the Block," 26
Smith, Bessie, 14, 113; biography of, 115
Smith, Mamie, 113
"Southern Mammy Sings," 43-44

Spanish Civil War, 73
Spenser, Edmund, 58
Stepto, Robert, 97-98
Stevens, Wallace, 45
"Strange Hurt," 42
Suitcase Theater (Harlem), 133 n 1
Sullivan, Noel, 104
"Sunset in Dixie," 80

Taylor, Edward, 45
Taylor, Patricia E., 17
technique: frozen sequence, 83; rhetorical address, 83; stream of consciousness, 82, 95
Tennyson, Alfred Lord, 58
theory, 83, 122
Thompson, Louise, 17, 24, 25
Thurman, Wallace, 17, 20
"To Captain Mulzac," 78
"To Hell with Dying," 65
tragedy: conventions, 100; sources, 118
tragi-comedy, 99-124
"Troubled Island," 133 n 2
"Troubled Woman," 2
"Trumpet Player: 52nd Street," (also "Trumpet Player") 63, 120
Turner, Darwin T., 132 n 1

unity: in vision and work, 32; unifying complexes, "Berry," 103; "Mother to Son," 36-39; "Negro Mother," 39-41
"Unquote," 21, 34

Van Vechten, Carl, 20
Velásquez, Diego, 73
Villard, Oswald, 11
Vivian G. Harsh Collection, 127
Voices, 33

Walker, A'lelia, 113; as entertainer of New Negroes, 12, 18
Walker, George, 15

Walker, Madam, 113
"wander," vs. "wonder," 10
"Water-Front Streets," 58
Ways of White Folks, The, 100, 104
"Weary Blues," 54, 63, 120; musical
  transcendence, 122
Weary Blues, 47-59, 65
West, Dorothy, 65
Wheatley, Phillis, 48
When Harlem Was in Vogue, 15
"Where? When? Which," 95

Whitman, Walt, 45, 48, 62, 65;
  tradition of, 13
"Who But the Lord," 38
Williams, Bert, 12, 16
Wimsatt, W.K., 9
"wonder," vs. "wander," 10
Woodson, Carter G., 16
World War II, 82, 123
Wright, Richard, 12
writer, as distiller and interpreter of
  history, 31